The Poetry of Piety

The Poetry of Piety

An Annotated Anthology of Christian Poetry

Ben Witherington III
and
Christopher Mead Armitage

Baker Academic
A Division of Baker Book House Co
Grand Rapids, Michigan 49516

Published by Baker Academic
a division of Baker Book House Company
P.O. Box 6287, Grand Rapids, MI 49516–6287

Printed in the United States of America

Library of Congress Cataloging-in-Publication Data

The poetry of piety : an annotated anthology of Christian poetry/ [selected and annotated by] Ben Witherington III and Christopher Mead Armitage.
   p.   cm.
   Includes bibiographical references and index.
   ISBN 0-8010-2286-X (paper)
   1. Christian poetry, English. 2. Christan poetry, American. 3. Christian poetry, English—History and criticism. 4. Christian poetry, American—History and criticism. I. Armitage, Christopher M. II. Witherington, Ben 1951– III. Title.
PR1195.C48 P66 2002
821.008′03823—dc21   2001037980

Every effort was made to ascertain the copyright status of every poem in this book. Any failure to give proper credit will be amended in subsequent printings of the book. The authors gratefully acknowledge the cooperation of those who helped to make this anthology possible:

Birney, Earle: "El Greco: *Espolio*" from *Fall by Fury* by Earle Birney, copyright © 1977 by McClelland and Stewart. Reproduced with the permission of the Estate of Earle Birney.

Eliot, T. S.: "Journey of the Magi" and "Choruses from 'The Rock'" from *Collected Poems 1909-1962* by T. S. Eliot, copyright 1936 by Harcourt, Inc., copyright © 1964, 1963 by T. S. Eliot. Reprinted by permission of Harcourt, Inc., and Faber and Faber Ltd.

Hughes, Langston: "Ballad of Two Thieves" from *The Collected Poems of Langston Hughes* by Langston Hughes, copyright © 1994 by The Estate of Langston Hughes. Used by permission of Alfred A. Knopf, a division of Random House, Inc.

Hughes, Ted: "Crow's Theology" from *Crow: From the Life and Songs of the Crow*, copyright © 1970 by Ted Hughes. Reprinted by permission of Faber and Faber Ltd.

Jennings, Elizabeth: "Meditation on the Nativity" from *Collected Poems* by Elizabeth Jennings, copyright ©

1986 by Carcanet. Reproduced with the permission of David Higham Associates.

Lewis, C. S.: "The Apologist's Evening Prayer" from *Poems* by C. S. Lewis, copyright © 1964 by the Executors of the Estate of C. S. Lewis and renewed 1992 by C. S. Lewis Pte. Ltd. Reprinted by permission of Harcourt, Inc., and The C. S. Lewis Company.

Newman, John Henry: "Lead Kindly Light" reprinted by permission of Paul Chavasse, Provost of the Birmingham Oratory.

Scott, F. R.: "Diagonals: Hands" from *Signature* by F. R. Scott, copyright © 1964 by F. R. Scott. Reprinted with the permission of William Toye, Literary Executor for the Estate of F. R. Scott.

Thompson, Francis: "The Hound of Heaven" and "The Kingdom of God" reprinted by permission of Oliver Hawkins, Literary Executor for the estate of Francis Thompson.

Updike, John: "Seven Stanzas at Easter" from *Collected Poems 1953-1993* by John Updike, copyright © 1993 by John Updike. Used by permission of Alfred A. Knopf, a division of Random House, Inc.

Wilbur, Richard: "Matthew VIII, 28ff." from *Walking to Sleep: New Poems and Translations*, copyright © 1969 by Richard Wilbur. Reprinted by permission of Harcourt, Inc., and Faber and Faber Ltd.

Contents

Introduction

Thousands of poems exist that express sentiments and ideas about Christ and Christian theology. Many of them are competently written but of no particular literary distinction, such as the metrically smooth hymns of the eighteenth and nineteenth centuries that continue to be popular, partly because of the tunes to which they have been set. For the most part, we have excluded that kind of verse, and we have not made excerpts from long poems such as *Paradise Lost*.

We took as a starting point the end of the sixteenth century. By that time, the English language was sufficiently settled in its modern form to be understandable to readers today with a minimum of explanatory notes. That era saw the great flowering of literature by Shakespeare and his contemporaries, and religious poetry flourished from the pens of John Donne, George Herbert, Robert Herrick, Henry Vaughan, and others till the middle of the seventeenth century. Subsequently, the mood and tone of religious poetry underwent various modulations, notably the increased expression of yearning in the nineteenth and twentieth centuries for lost certainties of belief. Our selection of poems reflects these changes.

The commentaries consist of a brief biographical note about each author, a section on the literary aspects of the poem, and a section titled "The Piety," which enlarges on the religious significance and relevance of the poem, especially for today's world.

We wish to thank Sue Nicholson for providing a good number of the questions for reflection and for her help in assembling the manuscript. We especially wish to thank Rhonda Hartweg, Ben's research assistant, for the many hours of work she spent in obtaining permission to use various poems. Finally, we are grateful to Darlene Hyatt for carefully proofreading the manuscript.

Ben Witherington III
and Christopher Mead Armitage

ONE

Sir Walter Ralegh
(1554–1618)

Sir Walter Ralegh is the epitome of the Renaissance man—multitalented, adventurous, and ambitious. He was, however, periodically in then out of favor with Queen Elizabeth, and during the reign of James I, Ralegh was charged with treason, sentenced to death, and beheaded. Like other courtiers of the period, he composed poems but did not bother to have them published as a collection.

Epitaph

Even such is Time, which takes in trust
Our youth, our joys, and all we have,
And pays us but with age and dust;
Who in the dark and silent grave,
When we have wandered all our ways,   5
Shuts up the story of our days.
But from which earth and grave and dust
The Lord shall raise me up, I trust.

The Poetry

Ralegh's poem was reputedly written in the front of his Bible the night before he was scheduled to be executed. Originally, the poem was the last stanza of his melancholy love poem "Nature, that washed her hands in milk," where it began "Oh, cruel Time!" and omitted the concluding couplet. These changes convert the poem from a despairing lament into a declaration of

Christian hope. This transformation is, however, in accord with the providential view of life that Ralegh expresses in other works, especially his *History of the World.*

The Piety

This brief epitaph focuses on the idea of exchange. What Time gives with the right hand, in due course it takes back with the left. To put it another way, personified time operates rather like the devil's instrument. The joys and excitements of youth are not given freely but are given only in "trust." They are not true gifts but rather loans for which Time will eventually require payment. Indeed, the payback comes in part by the aging process itself and more fully by death and disintegration in the grave. But in the end, Time does not have the last word for those who are in Christ. Ralegh concludes the poem by stressing that God will have the last word and will, in fact, reverse the ravages of death by means of the resurrection. God's yes is louder than Time's no. Thus, the "story of our days" has an epilogue without end. For those who share Ralegh's trust in the Lord of the resurrection, the final period of death becomes a comma.

Questions for Reflection

How would you characterize the story of your days so far?

What did you enjoy in previous years that has now disappeared?

What aspects of your life do you think will continue at the resurrection? What will cease (Rev. 21:1–4)?

Take a few moments to thank God for defeating death and to reflect on the promise of bodily resurrection.

TWO

John Donne
(1572–1631)

John Donne was born into a devout Roman Catholic family and was descended on his mother's side from Sir Thomas More, who was martyred in 1535 for adhering to that faith. In Donne's lifetime, a Jesuit uncle was sentenced to death but then exiled from England, and Donne's younger brother Henry, arrested for harboring a priest, died of the plague while in Newgate Prison. Donne left Oxford University without a degree, probably because graduation required conforming to the Church of England. During the 1590s, however, he aligned himself with the Protestant establishment by sailing on expeditions against the Spaniards and by writing a prose satire against the Jesuits (*Ignatius His Conclave*, 1611) and a treatise arguing that Catholics ought to take the oath of allegiance to the crown (*Pseudo-Martyr*, 1610). The latter gained Donne favor with King James I, who urged him to become a minister in the Church of England, which he finally did in 1615. Six years later, he was installed as dean of St. Paul's Cathedral. His sermons (of which over 160 survive) established his reputation as a great preacher. Like his poems, his sermons show vigorous language, daring arguments, and metaphorical inventiveness.

Holy Sonnet 7

At the round earth's imagined corners, blow
Your trumpets, angels, and arise, arise
From death, you numberless infinities
Of souls, and to your scattered bodies go,

11

All whom the flood did, and fire shall o'erthrow,   5
All whom war, dearth, age, agues, tyrannies,
Despair, law, chance, hath slain, and you whose eyes,
Shall behold God, and never taste death's woe.
But let them sleep, Lord, and me mourn a space,
For, if above all these, my sins abound,   10
'Tis late to ask abundance of thy grace,
When we are there; here on this lowly ground,
Teach me how to repent; for that's as good
As if thou hadst sealed my pardon, with thy blood.

The Poetry

This sonnet incorporates the three parts of the meditation.[1]
The first part, *composition of place,* is created by the speaker
mentally envisioning the end of the world in lines 1–4. Lines 5–
8 make up the second part, the *analysis.* All the dead and the living ("you whose eyes / Shall behold God, and never taste death's
woe") will come to judgment. The third part, the *colloquy* or
speaking with God, starts in line 9 and occupies the rest of the
sonnet. In lines 11–12, the speaker acknowledges it is too late for
repentance when one arrives at judgment ("there"). He begs to
be taught repentance here on earth. The final line uses the hypo-
thetical "as if," although Christian believers know that their par-
dons have been guaranteed ("sealed") by Christ's sacrifice.

The Piety

As with most of Donne's divine meditations, a healthy knowledge of the biblical subtexts or echoes enhances one's understanding of and reflection on the poem. The first line alludes to
Revelation 7:1, where John the seer writes of seeing four angels
standing at the earth's corners and holding back the winds. The
apostle also writes of another angel that has the seal of the living
God (v. 2), and he tells of the sealing of the servants of God on
their foreheads (v. 3). The image of sealing in the latter case has
to do with protecting the believers during the maelstrom that
will follow when the great tribulations preceding the final judgment are unleashed. Believers are not taken out of the world but

---

1. See pp. 27–28 below, on "Hymn to God, My God, in My Sickness."

are protected within it. Revelation 7:4 then goes on to speak of the specific number of the elect—144,000—symbolizing the full complement of the people of God (noting the multiple of twelve, the number for the tribes of Israel, and so of God's people).

Donne draws on these apocalyptic images to convey the notion of finality once the precursors to the last judgment ensue. At that time, it will be too late for repentance and amendment of life. In short, this life is the place for making decisions that will determine one's ultimate destiny in the afterlife. The motto "sin in haste, repent at leisure" is one that Donne encourages his readers to abandon. Donne sees final judgment as a day of reckoning, but it can also be a day of reconciliation if one prepares here and now.[2]

It is interesting how Donne combines what then amounted to "modern" cosmology with ancient Christian beliefs. On the one hand, he speaks of the earth's "imagined corners" (taking Revelation to be speaking figuratively) and of its roundness. On the other hand, he speaks of a literal resurrection where souls return to bodies, an event that happens "here on this lowly ground" (see 1 Cor. 15:51–52). Salvation is individual as each soul returns to its own body.

Unlike the fervent apostle John, who prays at the end of his Apocalypse "Amen. Lord Jesus, come soon," Donne prays for delay so there may be time for amendment of life. Notice that he asks to be taught how to repent—repentance being seen as a gift from God and not something that comes naturally to the sinner. An interesting juxtaposition of the subjective and objective benefits of Christ's death appears at the close of the sonnet. Christ's death enables repentance, which appropriates the pardon of God, the objective benefit of Christ's atoning death. Obviously, pardon offered and pardon received are viewed as two separate things. Donne was not one who believed that the benefits of Christ's death, however potentially universal in effect, were automatically applied without being received by faith with a penitent heart. The poet knows there are many ways to die, but he envisions only one way into eternal life. This sense of accountability and finality permeates the poem and leads the reader to reflection and circumspection.

2. This is a regular theme in Donne's divine poems. See "Hymn to God, My God, in My Sickness" (pp. 26–29).

Questions for Reflection

When do you think the final judgment will come?

Do you hope with the apostle John that the judgment will come soon or that there will be a delay? Why?

How would your daily walk with Christ change if you knew that Jesus Christ would be returning today?

What are the sins in your life that you need to bring before God in repentance?

Take a few minutes to reflect on repentance. Ask God to teach you how to repent.

Holy Sonnet 14

Batter my heart, three-personed God; for you
As yet but knock, breathe, shine, and seek to mend;
That I may rise, and stand, o'erthrow me, and bend
Your force, to break, blow, burn, and make me new.
I, like an usurped town, to another due,   5
Labour to admit you, but oh, to no end,
Reason your viceroy in me, me should defend,
But is captived, and proves weak or untrue,
Yet dearly I love you, and would be loved fain,
But am betrothed unto your enemy.   10
Divorce me, untie or break that knot again;
Take me to you, imprison me, for I,
Except you enthral me, never shall be free,
Nor ever chaste, except you ravish me.

The Poetry

Donne opens with a violent imperative that sets the tone he will sustain throughout the poem. The four verbs in line 2 are paired with four more intense forms of the same actions in line 4. All eight verbs create the image of God as a blacksmith hammering at his anvil and forge. A siege image dominates lines 5–8, and a third cluster of images involving sexual and marital violence follows in the sestet (lines 9–14). Collectively, these images express the speaker's sense of inadequacy and unworthiness and his vehement appeal to God to remake him.

In lines 5–8, the speaker compares himself to a town that owes allegiance to God but has been captured by the devil. Human reason, God's "viceroy," should defend the speaker but proves incapable or false. The poet declares his love for God and his ardent desire to be loved by the Lord (line 9), but he has been won by the enemy and cannot escape unless God captures him ("Except you enthral me" [line 13]). The final line presents an even more striking example of the paradoxes that Donne uses in the poem (lines 3, 12, 13, and 14).

The Piety

Donne clearly expresses that salvation is not a human self-help program. Human nature is fallen, and redemption comes only through drastic action by God. Radical transformation, not mere modification, is required if a human being is to be remade into the image of God. Donne was not an early advocate of the therapeutic model of redemption. Even more sobering is the fact that he speaks as a person who is not adamantly opposed to God; rather, he labors to admit God into his life. Even so, drastic action by God is required. In Donne's view, if one is not enthralled by God, one is the captive of the usurper. There is no middle ground. Reason is seen as no match for the powers of darkness.

This poem strongly suggests that salvation is not just a matter of knowing or even desiring the truth. It is also a matter of willing the good. However, the human will is portrayed as captive, bent, and fallen unless God remolds it, straightens it, and sets it upright. Information without transformation is inadequate. A change of mind is only the beginning; a change of heart is also required.

The poem's subject is reminiscent of the one who says "Lord, Lord" but does not do the master's will (Matt. 7:21). The speaker loves God but cannot be faithful unless God's love overpowers him so that all other alliances and allegiances are broken, dissolved, or put in their rightful places. Donne, then, is suggesting that the proper relationship with the Deity is an all-consuming need because of humanity's fallen condition. Donne's painful honesty about the waywardness of humanity demonstrates that his piety did not entail mere wishful thinking but faith in a reliable God. Yet it is obvious that Donne is not a pure fideist; he sees reason as God's assistant in human beings, although it is a weak and sometimes untrue assistant. Right reason and right feelings are good but insufficient. They must be complemented by a right will.

Donne's analysis implies that salvation is not just an event that happens to a person at conversion. Rather, an ongoing process of renovation, renewal, and remaking is necessary if the believer is to remain true to God throughout life. There is comfort in the opening lines, however, for they suggest that God, like the diligent blacksmith, is hard at work remaking his creatures. He will always respond to the impassioned prayers of those who desire his will for humankind.

Questions for Reflection

What areas of your life has God recently transformed and made anew? Take time to thank God for his work in these areas.

How does God use reason in your spiritual walk?

In what areas of your life is reason not enough? How has God been working to right your will in these areas?

Do you agree there can be no middle ground in your commitment to God? Why or why not?

Are there areas of your life where you feel captive to the usurper? Ask God to change your heart.

Holy Sonnet 15

I am a little world made cunningly
Of elements, and an angelic sprite,
But black sin hath betrayed to endless night
My world's both parts, and, oh, both parts must die.
You which beyond that heaven which was most high   5
Have found new spheres, and of new lands can write,
Pour new seas in mine eyes, that so I might
Drown my world with my weeping earnestly,
Or wash it, if it must be drowned no more:
But oh it must be burnt; alas the fire   10
Of lust and envy have burnt it heretofore,
And made it fouler; let their flames retire,
And burn me O Lord, with a fiery zeal
Of thee and thy house, which doth in eating heal.

The Poetry

In this sonnet, Donne utilizes several traditional ideas about the composition of human beings and the cosmos. Lines 1 and 2 refer to the theory that each person is a microcosm ("little world") consisting of the four elements (earth, water, air, and fire) and an angelic spirit or soul. Both body and soul are destined to die (line 4). "You" (line 5) may refer to astronomers such as Galileo. It could also refer to the blessed, who have ascended to a heaven beyond mortal estimate and, like new explorers, can write about their discoveries. The speaker implores them to provide "new seas" (line 7) of penitential tears in which he can drown the world or at least cleanse it of sin.

The speaker's tone changes at line 10 as he reflects that God's second destruction of the world will not be by flood but by fire. In the past, he has burned with the sins of lust and envy (line 11). Now he pleads that their flames will be replaced with God's fire, which paradoxically restores by destroying sin and enables him to be resurrected out of his ashes. The last two words of the poem perhaps also refer to partaking of the Eucharist.

The poem has one unusual feature of form. Although Donne adheres to the rhyme scheme of an Italian sonnet (*abbaabba cdcdee*), his syntax divides the poem into units of nine and five lines instead of the usual eight and six. Thus, Donne's poetic technique is both traditional and unorthodox.

The Piety

Donne, like many Christian authors through the ages, is fascinated by the correlation between a human being as a "little world" and the larger world itself. Christian ecological reflections emphasize that the fate of the microcosm and macrocosm stand or fall together. But long before the age of ecology, Donne is already meditating on such matters. He assumes the world will not experience a second flood of biblical proportions (see Gen. 9:11); rather, it faces a final eschatological conflagration (2 Pet. 3:10).

In order to reestablish fellowship with God, Donne must be cleansed as the world was in antiquity. He must also be purged of fire and by fire in preparation for the final purgation. The fires of his lust must recede while the fire of the Lord (i.e., zeal for

God and God's house) must blaze, burning away the blackness in his soul and thereby healing it.

It is worth reflecting on the fact that Donne anticipates that both the body and the "angelic sprite" must perish. He does not have in mind the Holy Spirit nor what we might call the soul. Rather, Donne is referring to the human spirit or life principle which, like breath or wind (the Greek word *pneuma* can mean all three), is part of the material world and not the eternal world. It is not clear from this poem whether Donne's theological anthropology distinguished the immortal soul from the spirit or life breath (see 1 Thess. 5:23). What is evident is Donne's belief that the saints, like Christ, are alive in heaven (lines 5–6) and have found a new world there with new lands and seas. They can assist Donne in his process of spiritual formation and renovation.

The last two lines of the poem involve a daring analogy, not because Donne compares himself to the psalmist (see Ps. 69:9) but because he may be comparing himself to Christ (see John 2:16–17). Like Donne, Christ also faced temptation, but he was aided by God to overcome wrong inclinations. If one is consumed with a passion for God and for God's people and work, other passions are burned up.

Questions for Reflection

Donne contrasts the fire of his sin with the fire of God. How are these fires similar? How are they different? What other images can you think of that convey a similar contrast?

Have you ever experienced a flood or seen a flood's destruction on TV? Reflect on the sin in your life, and imagine God's healing grace washing it away like a flood.

What "new lands" do you imagine exist in heaven?

When have you been most zealous for the Lord? What were the circumstances contributing to your fervor?

Take time to pray, and ask God to rekindle your zeal for him.

Holy Sonnet 19

Oh, to vex me, contraries meet in one:
Inconstancy unnaturally hath begot
A constant habit; that when I would not

I change in vows, and in devotion.
As humorous is my contrition   5
As my profane love, and as soon forgot:
As riddlingly distempered, cold and hot,
As praying, as mute; as infinite, as none.
I durst not view heaven yesterday; and today
In prayers, and flattering speeches I court God: 10
Tomorrow I quake with true fear of his rod.
So my devout fits come and go away
Like a fantastic ague: save that here
Those are my best days, when I shake with fear.

The Poetry

This sonnet abounds with paradoxes about human changeability. Donne laments his tendency to defeat his intentions,
whether religious ("humorous" in line 5 means "changeable,"
not comic) or secular (line 6). The syntax varies from the complete clauses in lines 1–6 to the compact phrases in lines 7–8.
Lines 9–10 start with "I durst not view heaven" but end with the
opposite, "I court God." Yesterday's emotions will be altered today, and tomorrow's will be different again. The speaker's religious moods ("devout fits") fluctuate like temperature changes
during a fever ("ague"); but in a final paradox, he declares that
his best days are when he trembles with fear of God.

The Piety

Hamlet states, "What a piece of work is a man." This poem
merely accentuates the point that humans are complex beings,
especially in their relationships with God. Donne depicts himself
as being like the apostle Peter, who exercised faith at one moment and feared the next (Matt. 14:28–30) or professed his un-
dying loyalty to Jesus only to deny him three times (Matt. 26:33–
34, 57–75). Donne says that the only thing permanent about his
relationship with God is its changeability.

Fearing God is not a topic we hear much about in churches
these days, but it has been a major emphasis in church history.
It was so important to John Knox that he inscribed the com-
mand "Fear God" on the lintel of his door in Edinburgh. The idea
of fear is not so much terror as profound awe and reverence for

God. Those who try to cozy up to him as a pal do not understand the nature of the biblical God. He is not a peer. No human being should try to relate to God as an equal. He is a holy and powerful being who must be respected. We respect a live 1,000-volt electrical wire. It is a powerful force that can do great good, but it can destroy us if we improperly relate to it. So it is in our relationship with the Almighty. As Jonathan Edwards once said, it is a fearful thing to come into the hands of an angry God.

Donne is dealing with a primal emotion when he speaks of fearing God. The days that he most fears God are his best days precisely because he relates to God as real and Almighty. That is, on those days he realizes his place in the divine scheme of things, and he understands the overwhelming power and reality that is God.

Something else is happening in this poem as well. Think for a moment of an occasion when people have been chasing you, and you are afraid of them. While you may not tremble when you are convinced they are far away, you are likely to do so when you hear their footsteps close at hand. Donne has heard the footsteps of the Almighty tracking him down, and he quakes at the prospect of having a close encounter with God. Paradoxically, he has been sending up his petitions to this same being. The nearness of God makes him tremble. Donne both desires and fears a close relationship with the Almighty. His fears are caused by memories of his past intemperance. But in this poem, Donne does not contemplate the ultimate paradox. The God who demands holiness of his children gives what he commands, and the God who commands love first offers it in the form of daily forgiveness.

Questions for Reflection

It has been said, "Blessed are those who expect nothing from God, for they will not be disappointed." What do you think John Donne expects of God in his present state? Do you think he was right to fear God? Why or why not?

Have you ever been afraid of God? Why? What is the difference between fearing and revering God?

Consider for a moment the inconsistencies in your Christian life. Write out a list of them, and ask yourself why you act and think and

pray in such an inconsistent pattern. Do you think you would do so
if you remained steadily aware that God is close at hand watching
you every moment of the day?

What do you think of Peter? Do you identify with him in his change-
ableness? Why or why not?

The Cross

Since Christ embraced the Cross itself, dare I
His image, th' image of his Cross deny?
Would I have profit by the sacrifice,
And dare the chosen altar to despise?
It bore all other sins, but is it fit   5
That it should bear the sin of scorning it?
Who from the picture would avert his eye,
How would he fly his pains, who there did die?
From me, no pulpit, nor misgrounded law,
Nor scandal taken, shall this Cross withdraw,   10
It shall not, for it cannot; for, the loss
Of this Cross, were to me another cross;
Better were worse, for, no affliction,
No cross is so extreme, as to have none.
Who can blot out the Cross, which th' instrument   15
Of God, dewed on me in the Sacrament?
Who can deny me power, and liberty
To stretch mine arms, and mine own cross to be?
Swim, and at every stroke, thou art thy cross,
The mast and yard make one, where seas do toss.   20
Look down, thou spiest out crosses in small things;
Look up, thou seest birds raised on crossed wings;
All the globe's frame, and sphere's, is nothing else
But the meridians crossing parallels.
Material crosses then, good physic be,   25
And yet spiritual have chief dignity.
These for extracted chemic medicine serve,
And cure much better, and as well preserve;
Then are you your own physic, or need none,
When stilled, or purged by tribulation.   30
For when that Cross ungrudged, unto you sticks,
Then are you to yourself, a crucifix.
As perchance, carvers do not faces make,

But that away, which hid them there, do take:
Let crosses, so, take what hid Christ in thee,   35
And be his image, or not his, but he.
But, as oft alchemists do coiners prove,
So may a self-despising, get self-love.
And then as worst surfeits, of best meats be,
So is pride, issued from humility,   40
For, 'tis no child, but monster; therefore cross
Your joy in crosses, else, 'tis double loss,
And cross thy senses, else, both they, and thou
Must perish soon, and to destruction bow.
For if th'eye seek good objects, and will take   45
No cross from bad, we cannot 'scape a snake.
So with harsh, hard, sour, stinking, cross the rest,
Make them indifferent; call nothing best.
But most the eye needs crossing, that can roam,
And move; to th' others th' objects must come home.   50
And cross thy heart: for that in man alone
Points downwards, and hath palpitation.
Cross those dejections, when it downward tends,
And when it to forbidden heights pretends.
And as the brain through bony walls doth vent   55
By sutures, which a cross's form present,
So when thy brain works, ere thou utter it,
Cross and correct concupiscence of wit.
Be covetous of crosses, let none fall.
Cross no man else, but cross thyself in all.   60
Then doth the Cross of Christ work fruitfully
Within our hearts, when we love harmlessly
That Cross's pictures much, and with more care
That Cross's children, which our crosses are.

The Poetry

"The Cross" exemplifies a kind of wit much admired in the seventeenth century. In the thirty-two rhyming couplets that make up this poem, the words *cross, crosses, crossing,* and *crossed* occur thirty-two times, and *crucifix* occurs once. Various meanings of *cross* are invoked, sometimes simultaneously. Among them are:

• the instrument of Christ's crucifixion (lines 1–8, 15, 32, 61)
• the gesture Christians make across their chests (line 51)

- any two objects that cross at right angles (lines 17–24)
- a burden (lines 14, 64)
- a frustration (line 14)
- an opposition (lines 41, 43–49, 58, 60).

Donne engages in this wordplay not solely for amusement but to bring out the hidden designs and correspondences in the divinely created world.

The first ten lines, especially lines 9–10, invoke a controversy between the Puritans and King James I. The Puritans thought that the Church of England had not been sufficiently reformed during the sixteenth century. From the pulpit, their preachers denounced representations of the cross as idolatrous and called making the sign of the cross a scandal. Its exclusion even from the baptismal service (line 16) was one of the demands in their Millenary Petition of 1603. The following year, however, at a conference in Hampton Court, the king rejected their demands. Donne's poem clearly supports the royal position.

Lines 26–30 draw on the medical theories of the day, which maintained that disease could be cured by employing antagonistic remedies. Donne argues that beneficial as material crosses are, spiritual ones are better. They are like chemically extracted medicines that cure and preserve. When distilled or purified, these medicines can be self-applied through suffering. If one applies them willingly, one becomes an image of Christ (lines 31–32, echoing lines 1–2). Lines 33–34 reiterate an idea articulated in a sonnet by Michelangelo. Just as the sculpture lies within the block of stone and waits to be uncovered, the Christian is latent within the human being. Lines 35–36 refer to alchemists who, having failed to purify base metals into gold, go to the opposite extreme of forging coins. Similarly, the deep humility Puritans professed often revealed their pride. Like Eve, if we rely solely upon our senses, we will fail to recognize the snake (line 46). All our senses need mortifying (lines 47–48), especially our eyes, which can roam around.

Lines 51–52 draw on Aristotle's observation that a human being is almost the only creature whose heart jumps in anticipation of the future. Donne suggests that the human heart pulls him downwards. But he should equally guard against "forbidden heights" (line 54) since the juncture of bones at the top of his skull form a cross that should restrain the temptation to indulge in excessive mental ingenuity (line 58). Some readers may consider that a poem metaphorically linking Christ's cross with swimming, ship design, birds, maps, medical cures, sculpture, alchemists' frauds, frustration of the senses, and cardiac impulses displays precisely the "concupiscence of wit" the poet declares should be corrected (line 58). The implicit and acknowledged egotism of such a parade of wit is mitigated, however, by his closing exhortation to live according to the central idea of Christianity.

The Piety

The naturalist John Muir once said that we look at life from the backside of the tapestry. Most of the time, we see only loose threads, knots, disconnected bits of matter. But, says Muir, when the sun shines through the tapestry, we get an occasional glimpse of the larger design, and we see that it is a matter of light and dark, joy and sorrow, all woven together into a beautiful pattern. John Donne clearly believes that the cross is one of those symbols or patterns that can be seen in nature as well as in human nature; in "His story" as well as in history. As such, it is a key to the meaning of life. Donne is not merely dealing with the paradoxical principle that in God's world the more we humble ourselves, the more we will be exalted. He is dealing with the fact that the life of Christ, or more particularly his death, provides a pattern for believers. We must also take up the cross and follow Christ.

However, we must not take up just any cross. As Mark 8:34 makes clear, self-denial and taking up one's *own* cross is the order of the Christian life. This entails the mortification of sinful desires and tendencies that Donne refers to in lines 50 and following. While Donne is most concerned with the "lust of the eye" and pride (see line 40), the devil is also mentioned indirectly in the reference to the snake (line 46). This unholy trinity of sin as recorded in 1 John 2:16 sums up what constitutes worldliness. It is contrasted with the statement, "We know love by this, that he laid down his life for us—and we ought to lay down our lives for one another" (1 John 3:16). In short, Christians are called to be cross bearers, not merely cross wearers, and we must cross out the selfish and self-indulgent tendencies that are antithetical to following Christ's example.

This poem is a potent reminder that there is no gospel of self-indulgence or health and wealth or conspicuous consumption, despite what is being preached from some pulpits today. Equally, I suggest that Donne is examining himself in this poem, for he knows he has just created something that could be considered a metaphysical conceit and thus an object of pride. Yet he crosses out such thoughts when he writes, "Cross no man else, but cross thyself in all" (line 60). In a sense, writing this poem is his own means of purgation. It reminds us that some spiritual disciplines are worth undertaking not because they are pleasant in themselves, but because they will lead to a better understanding of self. We are not the saviors of the world; that role can only be played by Christ. Yet it is possible for us to willingly make sacrifices so that we see ourselves in true perspective and also imitate the one to whom all lesser cross patterns point. Paradoxically, only a self-confident person is able to step down as Christ did and make sacrifices for others, however humiliating the act may be.

> The world is now left hanging
> Upon a crooked tree
> In Christ the microcosm
> Death and life for you and me.

Questions for Reflection

Look around and see how many images of the cross can be found in ordinary objects.

In what areas of your life are you especially proud? Thank God for the gifts he has given you.

In what areas does your pride have a tendency to go too far? Ask God to forgive you for self-indulgence.

What does taking up the cross of Christ mean for your life? What is Christ asking you to deny, to sacrifice, to crucify?

What spiritual disciplines do you need to embrace to help you lead the cross-driven life? Take a few moments to ask God to enable you in this venture.

Hymn to God, My God, in My Sickness

Since I am coming to that holy room
   Where, with Thy choir of saints for evermore
I shall be made Thy music, as I come
   I tune the instrument here at the door,
   And what I must do then, think here before.   5

Whilst my physicians by their love are grown
   Cosmographers,[3] and I their map, who lie
Flat on this bed, that by them may be shown
   That this is my southwest discovery,[4]
   Per fretum febris,[5] by these straits[6] to die,   10

I joy that in these straits I see my west;[7]
   For though their currents yield return to none,
What shall my west hurt me? As west and east
   In all flat maps (and I am one) are one,[8]
   So death doth touch the resurrection.   15

Is the Pacific Sea my home? Or are
   The eastern riches? Is Jerusalem?[9]
Anyan,[10] and Magellan, and Gibraltar,
   All straits, and none but straits, are ways to them,
   Whether where Japhet dwelt, or Cham, or Shem.   20

3. Cosmographers are geographers particularly skilled in mapping the heavens as well as the features of the earth.

4. The south is the latitude for heat, or in this case fever, and the west was seen as the region of decline due to the setting sun. In other words, Donne is intimating that he foresees this fever may lead to death and so to discovery of a passage to a new world.

5. "Through the straits of fever." See the explanation on page 27.

6. Throughout this section of the poem, there is a playing on the two possible means of strait: narrow difficult passages (e.g., the Straits of Magellan) or sufferings (e.g., he is in dire straits).

7. Again, "west" is a synonym for decline and death.

8. Donne refers to the fact that ancient mapmakers would often show a portion of the next continent on the extremities of a flat map. For example, the furthest point west would also appear in part at the east end of the map. The allusion is to the fact that west symbolizes death, and east symbolizes resurrection and Christ. When Donne reaches his west, he will in fact have reached his east—Christ and resurrection.

9. All of these locations were seen as metaphors or symbols for peace and joy.

10. This is an allusion to the strait that divided the western part of America from Asia.

We think that Paradise and Calvary,
    Christ's Cross and Adam's tree, stood in one place;[11]
Look Lord, and find both Adams met in me;
    As the first Adam's sweat surrounds my face,
    May the last Adam's blood my soul embrace.   25

So, in His purple wrapped receive me Lord,[12]
    By these His thorns give me His other crown;
And as to others' souls I preached Thy word,
    Be this my text, my sermon to mine own:
    Therefore, that He may raise, the Lord throws down.   30

The Poetry

In this poem, the speaker is sick and faces the prospect of dying. Izaak Walton, Donne's contemporary biographer, records that Donne wrote this hymn only eight days before his death in 1631. Another contemporary, Sir Julius Caesar, says the poem was written during Donne's severe illness of 1623, when he also produced his famous prose work, *Devotions upon Emergent Occasions*.

This "hymn" is an outstanding example of poetic adaptation of the meditation as described in the *Spiritual Exercises* of Ignatius of Loyola and other religious manuals of the sixteenth and seventeenth centuries. Through the image of a musician carefully tuning his instrument before joining other musicians, the first stanza presents the mental concentration required in preparation for the three main stages of the meditation. In other words, Donne interprets his suffering as a devotional exercise, much like prayer and fasting.

The first stage is *composition of place*, and it is achieved by evoking a scene from the life of Christ or arousing a sense of one's personal involvement in a religious experience. In this poem, Donne develops an elaborate image of his bedridden, fatally sick self as a map, pored over by mapmakers (his physicians). The Latin phrase combines the meaning "by the heat of fever" and "by these dangerous straits" through which he must pass to his west (death).

11. This alludes to an idea found in a variety of medieval sources, in particular the Golden Legend, which suggested that Eden and Calvary were at the same spot and that Christ and Adam were buried at the same location.
12. Again, a double entendre. Purple is the color of the fevered Donne but also of Christ's saving royal blood. It may also be an allusion to his royal garb in which he wraps the saved sinner and so provides a unique burial shroud.

The second stage of the meditation, *analysis*, is seen in lines 11 through 22. The speaker rejoices at the prospect of dying, because as west and east ultimately meet, so his death is the necessary prelude to his resurrection. The fourth stanza suggests that wherever paradise may be—in Europe, Africa, or Asia (represented by Japheth, Ham, and Shem, the three sons of Noah)—the only way of getting there is through dangerous straits such as the Bering Straits (Anyan), the Straits of Magellan, or the Strait of Gibraltar.

The medieval tradition that the tree of knowledge and Christ's cross were located in the same spot leads into the third stage of the meditation, the *colloquy*. Here the speaker talks with God, as signified by a switch to second person in line 23 ("Look"). Donne prays to be wrapped in the royal purple, the blood of Christ's sacrifice, which will redeem him. Lines 28 and 29 allude to Donne's preaching career as dean of St. Paul's Cathedral in London. The final line reiterates the central paradox of the poem, that one's life must be lost in order to be saved.

Finally, note the basic rhyme scheme in the five line stanzas: *ababb*. In some cases, we are dealing with sight rhyme rather than aural rhyme (e.g., crown, own, down), and in other cases we are dealing with approximate rhyme (e.g., room/come or west/east). Donne is clearly more concerned with the consonance and fitness of ideas than of sounds.

The Piety

This poem, so rich in theological and geographical images, is a reflection of seventeenth- and eighteenth-century piety, which often focused on adequate spiritual preparation for death. Jeremy Taylor's classic *Holy Living and Holy Dying* reflects the same approach we find in this poem. The piety is thoroughly medieval in that it associates the recovery of Eden and resurrection with heaven, not with some series of earthly events following the second coming of Christ. Equally medieval and in line with Thomas à Kempis's *The Imitation of Christ* is the notion that Christ's sufferings are recapitulated in the life and death of the believer. This is not so much a matter of human imitation of Christ as divine duplication of a pattern.

Notice the allusion to "His thorns" in the final stanza. As in the life of Saint Paul (see 2 Cor. 12:7), it was God who sent this thorn to Donne, and ultimately it would be to his benefit by leading him to Eden and resurrection. In light of this, Donne sees it as his task to prepare for "holy dying" and not to rail against the dying of the light. We may also note the reference to Christ as the last Adam in the fifth stanza. Christians not only bear the image and fallenness of the first Adam; they also bear the image and new life of the second Adam. The effects of the fall and the effects of redemption meet in one person at death.

Finally, it is interesting to note the two ways that Donne uses the word *soul* in lines 25 and 28. The first reference is to the spiritual dimension of the human being, which was thought to go to heaven at death. Again, this idea is thoroughly medieval and reflects the effect of Greek thinking about body-soul dualism. The biblical idea as presented in the New Testament is of the inner person and the outer person or the human spirit and the human body. Donne's second reference to *soul* is much closer to this New Testament idea, for here the term refers to persons as whole or living beings to whom Donne had preached. This is close to Paul's use of the Greek word *psyche* in 1 Corinthians 15:45. The apostle quotes Genesis 2:7, which refers to Adam becoming "a living being" (in older translations, "a living soul"). In any event, the poem portrays the afterlife as a condition in which there will be no more suffering or sorrow but only joy and peace.

Questions for Reflection

Have you ever been so sick as to fear you were at the point of death? What were your reflections on God at the time? What effect has your recovery had on these reflections?

What "straits" (difficult passages) in your life must you go through to reach a place of peace and joy?

Reflect on one of the "thorns" in your life. How may God be using it to your benefit? Take time to thank God for these benefits.

How have you experienced the coming together of the first and last Adam in your life (sin and grace)?

Try using the structure of meditation outlined here to spend time with God. Begin by concentrating on a particular aspect of your life that you would like to bring before him. Next, think of an image—either a scene from the life of Christ or an analogy from your own experience—and reflect on this mental picture. Analyze the various aspects of this image. Finally, speak with God about your reflections.

THREE

Robert Herrick
(1591–1674)

Robert Herrick was the seventh child of a London goldsmith who died when Robert was only a year old. At 16, Robert was apprenticed to his uncle, also a goldsmith. Eventually released from the apprenticeship, in 1613 Robert entered Cambridge University, receiving a bachelor's degree in 1617 and a master's degree in 1620. In 1623 he was ordained as a priest in the Church of England. He served as an army chaplain on the disastrous expedition of 1627 to aid French Protestants in La Rochelle. He was rewarded with the living of Dean Prior in Devonshire and was installed as its vicar in 1630.

Accustomed to the company of the London school of poets surrounding Ben Jonson, Herrick was frequently frustrated by rural life. Yet, he also grew to appreciate rural customs such as May Day and harvest festivals, which the Puritans were trying to suppress. Herrick's Royalist sympathies led to his being ejected from his living in 1647 and his returning to London. The following year *Hesperides*, his 1,130 secular poems, and *Noble Numbers*, his 272 religious poems, were published together. When the monarchy was restored in 1660, Herrick was reappointed to his living in Devonshire, where he died.

To Keep a True Lent

Is this a fast, to keep
The larder lean,
And clean
From fat of veals and sheep?

Is it to quit the dish 5
    Of flesh, yet still
        To fill
The platter high with fish?

Is it to fast an hour
    Or ragg'd to go, 10
        Or show
A downcast look, and sour?

No; 'tis a fast to dole
    Thy sheaf of wheat
        And meat 15
Unto the hungry soul.

It is to fast from strife,
    From old debate
        And hate;
To circumcise thy life; 20

To show a heart grief-rent;
    To starve thy sin,
        Not bin.
And that's to keep thy Lent.

The Poetry

In this poem, Robert Herrick uses his poetic skill to renew a traditional topic. The quatrains have a most unusual visual arrangement and a count of six, four, two, and six syllables. The rhetoric of the poem is also balanced. Three quatrains pose questions, and three make assertions. The poem culminates in a triumphant last line.

The Piety

The notion of inward versus outward piety is a theme that resonates throughout Scripture, especially in the prophetic tradition (see Amos 5:21–24) and in various portions of the New Testament. Herrick might have been influenced in part by Isaiah 58:4–7, which reads,

Look, you fast only to quarrel and to fight and to strike with a wicked fist. Such fasting as you do today will not make your voice heard on high. Is such the fast that I choose, a day to humble oneself? Is it to bow down the head like a bulrush, and to lie in sackcloth and ashes? Will you call this a fast, a day acceptable to the LORD? Is not this the fast I choose: to loose the bonds of injustice, to undo the thongs of the yoke, to let the oppressed go free, and to break every yoke? Is it not to share your bread with the hungry, and bring the homeless poor into your house; when you see the naked, to cover them, and not to hide yourself from your own kin?

But this is a contrast between ritualistic religion and the practice of justice and mercy—two forms of outward piety.

Perhaps more influential is a text like Romans 2:29: "A person is a Jew who is one inwardly, and real circumcision is a matter of the heart—it is spiritual and not literal. Such a person receives praise not from others but from God." This gets at the essential inner/outer contrast Herrick has in mind. Fasting from physical food, or more specifically certain types of food (veal as opposed to fish, which is deemed acceptable during the fast), is not what true Lent keeping is all about. Nor is preserving a severe outward demeanor the heart of the matter. Rather, outward abstinence is meant to provide more space and time for concentrating on nourishment of the soul. Outward fasting and contrition are not pointless. They are the means to feeding a hungry spirit. Fasting is not an end in itself, and it is certainly no substitute for the true end.

Herrick is not offering an antiritual diatribe; he is making clear the essentials of the Lenten season. For instance, Lent is a time to circumcise our lives from strife and hate and contentiousness and to earnestly repent of our sin. Indeed, it is a season when sin is to go unfulfilled, not our stomachs. Herrick's complaint is not unlike that of Richard Baxter in *The Reformed Pastor*. Baxter writes of ministers who are careful in what they say from the pulpit and how they say it but who are careless in how they actually believe and live. For Herrick, the heart of religion is the religion of the heart. If the heart is transformed and right with God, then right actions and proper acts of worship will flow from it. If our hearts are not right with God and are not the focus of our contrition and atonement, we have missed the point. The days may lengthen (the notion from which the term *Lenten* comes), but wisdom and intimacy with the Almighty will not increase in breadth and intensity.

Questions for Reflection

Have you ever fasted for Lent or known someone who did? What did this fast consist of? What spiritual insights did you gain?

When have you had the greatest spiritual insights in your life—when you were well off or in deep need?

What area of your soul is "hungry" and in need of God's "sheaf of wheat / and meat"?

In what areas do you need to circumcise sin from your life?

If you are physically able, commit to a 24-hour fast sometime this week. Try to schedule it during a time when you have few other commitments so you can spend a significant amount of time in prayer and reflection. Write about your experience. (If your health prohibits this kind of fast, try another kind of fast [e.g., from TV or from work].)

His Litany to the Holy Spirit

In the hour of my distress,
When temptations me oppress,
And when I my sins confess,
    Sweet Spirit, comfort me!

When I lie within my bed,   5
Sick in heart and sick in head,
And with doubts discomforted,
    Sweet Spirit, comfort me!

When the house doth sigh and weep,
And the world is drowned in sleep,   10
Yet mine eyes the watch do keep,
    Sweet Spirit, comfort me!

When the artless doctor sees
No one hope, but of his fees,
And his skill runs on the lees,   15
    Sweet Spirit, comfort me!

When his potion and his pill
Has or none or little skill,
Meet for nothing but to kill,
    Sweet Spirit, comfort me!   20

When the passing bell doth toll,
And the furies in a shoal
Come to fright a parting soul,
    Sweet Spirit, comfort me!

When the tapers now burn blue,   25
And the comforters are few,
And that number more than true,
    Sweet Spirit, comfort me!

When the priest his last hath prayed,
And I nod to what is said,   30
'Cause my speech is now decayed,
    Sweet Spirit, comfort me!

When, God knows, I'm tossed about,
Either with despair or doubt,
Yet, before the glass be out,   35
    Sweet Spirit, comfort me!

When the Tempter me pursu'th
With the sins of all my youth,
And half damns me with untruth,
    Sweet Spirit, comfort me!   40

When the flames and hellish cries
Fright mine ears and fright mine eyes,
And all terrors me surprise,
    Sweet Spirit, comfort me!

When the Judgment is revealed,   45
And that opened which was sealed,
When to Thee I have appealed,
    Sweet Spirit, comfort me!

The Poetry

In "His Litany to the Holy Spirit," Robert Herrick takes the traditional litany, a form in which prayers are recited alternately by the
clergy and the congregation, and modifies it to make it "his." Each
stanza consists of a rhyming triplet and the refrain. The lines are
unusual in having an odd number of syllables—seven in the triplet

and five in the refrain—which may heighten the incantatory effect. In the fourth stanza, the doctor is "artless" because he lacks ability in curing, and the phrase "his skill runs on the lees" means his skill is drained to the last drops. In the seventh stanza, "The tapers now burn blue" signifies that evil spirits are present.

The Piety

In this poem, the author works through a catalog of potential disasters: temptation, doubt, insomnia, physical illness, death, hell, and final judgment. In each case, his recourse is to cry out for comfort from *the* comforter—the Holy Spirit. Notice that the poet does not request that he be spared the vicissitudes of life and fears about the afterlife. Rather, he asks for succor from the Spirit so that he may prevail in the face of such difficulties. In other words, he does not ask for a life that is equal to his own strengths and abilities but for divine assistance to deal with whatever life may bring him. Herein lies the mature Christian's approach to life.

While some people might read this litany as the cries of a weak and insecure person, such a conclusion would likely be wide of the mark. It is a sign of wisdom when a person realizes the need for outside assistance—indeed, divine assistance—to get through life's difficulties. When accused of leaning on God as a crutch in times of trouble, the mature Christian will respond that God is not merely a crutch or a bridge over troubled waters. Rather, God is our total support, the very foundation on which we stand whether the difficulties are little or large. Clearly, Herrick believes this. God is not merely the person Herrick turns to when all else fails. Rather, the Spirit is the source of comfort he turns to as a first, middle, and last resort—"a very present help in times of trouble."

Questions for Reflection

Which of the distresses listed (temptation, doubt, insomnia, sickness, death, fear of hell, final judgment) do you struggle with the least? The most?

How has the Spirit offered you comfort in the past?

When are you most quick to turn to God? When do you try to do things on your own?

Take time now to turn over all your weaknesses and fears to God and
to pray for the comfort of the Spirit.

His Saviour's Words, Going to the Cross

Have, have ye no regard, all ye
Who pass this way, to pity me
Who am a man of misery?

A man both bruis'd, and broke, and one
Who suffers not here for mine own   5
But for my friends' transgression?

Ah! Sion's Daughters, do not fear
The Cross, the Cords, the Nails, the Spear,
The Myrrh, the Gall, the Vinegar,

For Christ, your loving Savior, hath   10
Drunk up the wine of God's fierce wrath;
Only, there's left a little froth,

Less for to taste, than for to shew
What bitter cups had been your due,
Had He not drank them up for you.   15

The Poetry

Herrick imagines Christ commenting on his crucifixion and
its significance as it takes place. In the first two triplets, Christ
speaks in the first person. After the third triplet, which focuses
on the objects used to torment him, he changes to third person
in the last two triplets. That transition brings out his transformation from a suffering individual expressing sentiments that bor-
der on self-pity, to the Savior who chidingly explains how his
self-sacrifice appeases God's wrath.

The Piety

Herrick's profound meditation on God's wrath, placed in the
mouth of Christ himself, has significant echoes of Lamentations 1,
which speaks of Jerusalem deserted after the exile, its people in

mourning because God has brought judgment on the Holy City. Lamentations 1:12 says, "Is it nothing to you, all you who pass by? Look and see if there is any sorrow like my sorrow, which was brought upon me, which the Lord inflicted on the day of his fierce anger." In Herrick's poem, the words of mother Zion become the words of Christ himself. He faces a fate similar to that of the Holy City, for he too is about to endure the judgment of God. Another allusion is to Isaiah 51:17, which again speaks of Jerusalem facing God's wrath: "Rouse yourself, rouse yourself! Stand up, O Jerusalem, you who have drunk at the hand of the Lord the cup of his wrath, who have drunk to the dregs the bowl of staggering."

There is a certain oddity about the first two stanzas, for Christ seems to be complaining and soliciting sympathy, which is very different from the New Testament portrayal. On the other hand, the pathos of the poem is built around Christ's suffering for the sins of his friends and the reference to him as the loving Savior.

Perhaps the most interesting notion in the poem is that while Christ endured the vast majority of God's wrath in our stead, he did not endure it all. The wrath of God we do experience reminds us of what we should have endured if God had been merely just with humankind. But we might ask, if Christ's death was sufficient for the sins of the world and efficient for all those who believe in him, why should the believer even expect or be required to taste the "froth" from God's cup of wrath?

Herrick conjures up a God that many modern persons find unfathomable—a God of righteous anger. In a world of irresponsibility and no-fault everything (from insurance to divorces to automobile accidents), it is not surprising that the concept of a God who holds humans accountable for their actions is unpalatable. Even some theologians find the notion of God requiring his Son to die on a cross to be so offensive that they have labeled it the ultimate example of child abuse. We would much rather deal with an infinitely inoffensive deity who offers only love and reassurance, not one who exacts punishment for sin from us or from his innocent Son. Yet this entire line of thinking ignores that one of the dominant portrayals of God in both the Old and New Testaments is of a holy, righteous, and just God who can have no fellowship with darkness. If such a God was also loving and wanted to have fellowship with those who dwell in darkness, the sin problem had to be dealt with.

Christ's death was the one necessary and sufficient means of dealing with the sin problem. Far from being an example of child abuse, the cross is the ultimate emblem of God's love for humanity, an emblem of God's not wanting humankind to have to drink the cup of his wrath. Herrick's poem reminds us that when we say God is love, we must always qualify that remark by saying God is holy love, for God is not an infinitely indulgent parent who spoils his children. Christ's compassion in draining the cup for us is matched by God's passion in dealing with the sin problem and making eternal fellowship between himself and the divine image bearers possible.

Questions for Reflection

Take a few moments to imagine, like Herrick, what it must have been like for Christ to endure scourging, scorn, and crucifixion. What would be your thoughts if you chose to die for the crimes of another?

When you think of God, what description comes to mind?

Read Romans 2:5–11 and 8:37–39. How do these verses describe God?

Reflect on the "bitter cup" that Christ drank for you. Take time to thank him for his willingness to die so that you would not have to fear "the Cross, the Cords, the Nails, the Spear, / The Myrrh, the Gall, the Vinegar."

FOUR

George Herbert
(1593–1633)

Born in the county of Montgomery in Wales, George was the fifth son of Richard and Magdalen Herbert. When George was three, his father died. His mother was well known as a patron of John Donne and other poets. Educated at Westminster School and Trinity College, Cambridge, George was elected a fellow of Trinity in 1616, reader in rhetoric in 1618, and public orator of the university in 1620. The last position was regarded as a step toward a career at court, as was his representing Montgomery in Parliament in 1624–25. By 1628, however, he resigned as orator, and having already become a canon of Lincoln Cathedral in 1626, he was ordained as an Anglican priest in 1630. He ministered to a tiny rural parish in Bemerton near Salisbury until his death in 1633. In addition to one volume of poems, *The Temple* (1633), Herbert left a prose account of the model country parson, *A Priest to the Temple* (1652), and some translations.

Prayer (I)

Prayer the Church's banquet, angels' age,
   God's breath in man returning to his birth,
   The soul in paraphrase, heart in pilgrimage,
The Christian plummet sounding heav'n and earth;
Engine against th' Almighty, sinners' tower,   5
   Reversèd thunder, Christ-side-piercing spear,
   The six-days' world transposing in an hour,
A kind of tune, which all things hear and fear;

Softness, and peace, and joy, and love, and bliss,
   Exalted manna, gladness of the best,   10
   Heaven in ordinary, man well dressed,
The milky way, the bird of Paradise,
   Church-bells beyond the stars heard, the soul's blood,
   The land of spices; something understood.

The Poetry

Deceptive in its adherence to the rhyme scheme of a Shakespearean sonnet, this poem is unorthodox from a literary point of
view. It consists entirely of a series of descriptions of prayer, separated by commas, without a main verb or predication as ex-
pected in formal discourse. The range of metaphor is remarkable,
with several links emerging. One of these is the idea of prayer as
food: "banquet" (line 1), "manna" (line 10), "spices" (line 14).
Other metaphors include prayer as breath (line 2), enlarged
speech ("paraphrase" [line 3]), or music ("tune" [line 8]; "transposing" [line 7]; "church-bells" [line 13]). Metaphors of violence
dominate lines 6 and 7, "engine" being a tower used in siege warfare. Heavenly attributes fill lines 9 and 11. The final two words
make a striking conclusion, whether interpreted as an under-
statement acknowledging the infiniteness of prayer and the im-
possibility of defining it completely or as a declaration that its
wide-ranging significance has been grasped. As in all of Herbert's
poems, biblical and theological allusions underlie his words.

The Piety

Though most Christians today might think of prayer as a simple matter of petitioning the Almighty, it is clear that Herbert
sees it as far more. For one thing, he sees prayer as communion
with God and therefore something of a feast. Even if we do not
get what we ask for, in a sense we always get what is most
needed, namely, a drawing closer to God. The poet also sees
prayer as the natural spiritual response of human beings created
in God's image. It is like breath returning to its ultimate source,
and as such it helps resuscitate the breather. Finally, Herbert
sees real prayer as the distillation of what is truly on our minds
or in our hearts. It's as if our hearts are setting out on a journey
toward God (line 3); we pour out our very life blood. Prayer,
then, is a sort of spiritual sacrifice offered up to God.

Perhaps the most daring portion of the poem comes in lines 4–6 where Herbert alludes to the Tower of Babel, humanity's attempt to reach heaven on its own terms. Prayer is a chastened form of such an attempt that brings forth not God's judgment but God's succor. Prayer sounds out or takes measure of the will of the Almighty (line 4). It is like a tower erected to get the Almighty to capitulate on some subject. In line 6, Herbert suggests that prayer can pierce God like lightning and cause him to release a blessing. Even more daring is his comparing prayer to the spear that pierced Christ. This last is a reference to the medieval interpretation of John 19:34 that saw the blood and water coming from Christ's side as an allusion to the sacraments of the Lord's Supper and baptism (see Durer's famous woodcut of this scene where a communion chalice is held up to catch the blood and a small font to catch the water). Thus, Herbert suggests it is through prayer that we obtain the benefits of Christ's death.

Another of the many images in this poem conveys the idea that prayer can sum up the trials and tribulations of the week in a short span. It is also suggested that prayer, being powerful, is something human beings instinctively do but also fear. Beware of what you pray for; you may receive it. In line 11, prayer is compared to a garment that clothes us and makes us presentable before God, rather like spiritual fig leaves.

In the end, Herbert intimates that prayer is more than importuning. It is an opportunity to better understand God's will, to be fed, and to find contentment in knowing that things will turn out for the best. Thus, it produces gladness, peace, joy, and love as we recognize that we have been constantly receiving exalted manna, albeit unaware much of the time. Herbert alludes to the Good News at the end of the poem, where we are reminded that when prayer, like a church bell, peals out to God, it is most certainly heard.

Questions for Reflection

Reflect on the images of prayer as food (e.g., banquet, manna, spices). What does this communicate to you about the value of prayer?

Reflect on the images of violence used for prayer. What does this communicate to you about the power and passion of prayer?

Which of these images most reflects your view of prayer?

Which image is the most revolutionary or challenging to your view of prayer? Why?

Choose one of these images of prayer—one that is a new concept for you—and reflect on its meaning. Then spend time in prayer, experiencing this new meaning.

Denial

When my devotions could not pierce
    Thy silent ears,
Then was my heart broken, as was my verse;
    My breast was full of fears
        And disorder.   5

My bent thoughts, like a brittle bow,
    Did fly asunder.
Each took his way; some would to pleasures go,
    Some to the wars and thunder
        Of alarms.   10

As good go anywhere, they say,
    As to benumb
Both knees and heart, in crying night and day,
    "Come, come, my God, O come,"
        But no hearing.   15

Oh that Thou shouldst give dust a tongue
    To cry to Thee,
And then not hear it crying! All day long
    My heart was in my knee,
        But no hearing.   20

Therefore my soul lay out of sight,
    Untuned, unstrung;
My feeble spirit, unable to look right,
    Like a nipped blossom hung
        Discontented.   25

O cheer and tune my heartless breast,
    Defer no time;
That so Thy favors granting my request,
    They and my mind may chime,
        And mend my rhyme.   30

The Poetry

This poem exemplifies the poet's wit as he plays with the verse form to a serious end. Herbert's unusual stanzas rhyme *ababc*. The final line of each stanza stands out because it is unrhymed and short, containing just four syllables (including "of alarms" in line 10 since "alarms" was often pronounced "alarums," meaning a call to battle). The speaker's "disorder" is seen in his failure to rhyme fully. In the fourth stanza, he complains that God created humans out of dust but now apparently refuses to listen to them, even when they are on their knees in prayer. The poet's inability to reach God is continually emphasized, especially by the words "untuned, unstrung" in line 22. But even as he pleads, God grants his prayer. This is signified by the rhyming of lines 29 and 30, which bring the poem to tuneful closure.

The Piety

Some of Herbert's most poignant poems are on prayer (see above, "Prayer I"). Like the psalmist (e.g., Pss. 43, 51, 54), Herbert wrestles with the fact that he is in difficulties and that, even though he prays, God does not seem to hear, much less answer. Herbert shows a boldness in prayer, at one point even suggesting it was counterproductive for God to give human beings tongues if he is only going to turn a deaf ear to their cries for help. Yet, as the last two lines of the poem suggest, Herbert understands that the real problem is not God's unresponsiveness. Rather, his own prayer is like singing out of tune. We must pray in tune, aligned with God's will, if we want results, or we are bound to be frustrated.

Why is it we so often assume God does not answer our prayers, when in fact God's answer might well be no? No is indeed an answer to prayer, and it may suggest that we have not prayed aright in the first place. As this poem implies, God's response to prayer is not necessarily affected by our degree of earnestness or amount of importuning. If we pray for something that is not in accord with God's will, we can spend ever so much time kneeling and praying earnestly ("All day long / My heart was in my knee" [line 19]), but to no avail. God is not at our beck and call. We cannot twist God's arm and force the Almighty to do something he would otherwise not do. Nevertheless, we have a compassionate God who hears and is always ready to respond to our needs. We must keep in mind, however, that what we want is not always what we need. God responds at the point of our needs, not necessarily at the point of our requests.

Questions for Reflection

Reflect on a time when you prayed earnestly but felt like God did not answer you. How did you respond?

When do you feel closest to God in prayer?

How do you discern God's will?

How in tune with God's will is your life right now?

Ask God to tune your "heartless breast" and bring you in alignment with his will.

The Collar

I struck the board and cried, "No more!
I will abroad.
What? shall I ever sigh and pine?
My lines[1] and life are free; free as the road,
Loose as the wind, as large as store.[2]   5
Shall I be still in suit?[3]
Have I no harvest but a thorn
To let me blood, and not restore
What I have lost with cordial[4] fruit?
Sure there was wine   10
Before my sighs did dry it: there was corn
Before my tears did drown it.
Is the year only lost to me?
Have I no bays[5] to crown it?
No flowers, no garlands gay? all blasted?   15
All wasted?
Not so, my heart: but there is fruit,
And thou hast hands.
Recover all thy sigh-blown age
On double pleasures: leave thy cold dispute   20

1. Direction or lines of verse.
2. Plenty; abundance.
3. Petitioning, but Herbert may also mean clerical garb.
4. A cordial was medicine good for the heart.
5. Symbol of triumph, such as a laurel wreath.

Of what is fit and not. Forsake thy cage,
        Thy rope of sands,
Which petty thoughts have made, and made to thee
        Good cable, to enforce and draw,
                And be thy law,   25
        Whilst thou didst wink and wouldst not see.
                Away! Take heed!
                I will abroad.
Call in thy death's head[6] there: tie up thy fears.
                He that forbears   30
        To suit and serve his need,
                Deserves his load."
But as I rav'd and grew more fierce and wild
                At every word,
        Methoughts I heard one calling, "Child!"   35
        And I repli'd, "My Lord."

The Poetry

In this dramatic poem, the speaker argues internally about subjecting himself to Christian discipline. His first four words declare a rejection of Holy Communion (Herbert's contemporaries would take "board" to mean the communion table), as do lines 10–12 ("corn" is a British term for wheat). The speaker's rebellious frustration reverberates through the rhetorical questions in lines 3–16 and the seemingly confident assertions and exclamations in lines 17–32. But in lines 33–34, he recognizes his petulant and irrational actions, and his tirade is interrupted by a voice uttering the potent monosyllable, "Child!" The uncertainty of "Methoughts I heard one calling" leaves open whether God utters the word or whether the speaker is checked from within. In any case, the admonition and expression of paternal concern lead him to acknowledge his heavenly Father with the last two words of the poem.

Herbert skillfully replicates the speaker's anger by using staccato sentences, short lines, and an irregular rhyme scheme. The comparison of self-imposed discipline to a "rope of sands, / Which petty thoughts have made, and made to thee / Good cable, to enforce and draw" is a particularly apt metaphor. Finally, the poem's title is a play on words. A collar is a yoke but is also an

---

6. A human skull, a reminder of death.

item of clerical garb. *Collar* sounds like *choler,* meaning anger, and it also hints at the "caller" of line 35.

The Piety

On the surface, this poem seems to be about Herbert's struggle with the constraints of ministry and how those constraints prevent him from enjoying life to the fullest. The poem could also be read as Herbert's struggles with temptation of various sorts as supported by the reference to "double pleasures" in line 20. His sighing and pining betray the desire to indulge in various activities that would violate his clerical vows (lines 11 and 19).

While such an interpretation is plausible, it neglects the poet's allusions to communion as well as the whole tradition of penitential disciplines that precede the taking of communion, particularly in the Anglican and Catholic traditions. In this light, the sighs and tears have to do not with lusts but with penitential acts in preparation for taking communion. Herbert's rebellion, then, is not primarily against the ministerial call but against the acts of repentance for deeds that he would like to commit again, recovering his "sigh-blown age" (line 19).

Throughout the poem, Herbert portrays himself as a petulant child who resists what appear to be arbitrary rules and petty thoughts that constrain his behavior. Perhaps Herbert is commenting on the medieval monastic tradition that insisted on having a celibate clergy. More certainly, he is dealing with the medieval tradition of mortification of the flesh in preparation for communion. This tradition involved not only repentance of sins but also fasting, weeping, and in some cases physical beating. The reference to a thorn that lets him bleed (lines 7–8) may be more than a metaphor, as may the reference to medicine or cordials for self-inflicted lacerations (line 9). Herbert implies that abstinence simply makes the heart grow fonder; it does not deal with the root of the problem.

Whether Herbert's rebellion is directed primarily against the inherent sexual and social constraints of ministry or the particular constraints of the penitential disciplines, it is clear that he wrestles with the medieval model of piety where sexual and physical impulses, including the enjoyment of food, were seen as less than edifying, especially for a minister. This poem, then, provides a powerful opportunity to wrestle with the relationship between spirituality, sexuality, and the need for repentance and communion with God.

What forms should penitence take? How does one prepare for communion? Must the clergy abstain from sexual relations and the general pleasures of life in order to be holy? Apparently, Herbert is tempted to think otherwise. In him we see some of the first attempts to get beyond the medieval model of piety and purity. These attempts would come to fruition in the Puritans and in later Anglican traditions. In any event, we are reminded at the poem's end that, whatever our ravings, God will call us back to a right mind about such matters. With Herbert, we should be prepared to respond to God's chastening call. He stands with figures such as Samuel, who as a child responded properly to such a call (see 1 Sam. 3). The subject of this poem, therefore, is not ministerial burnout but ministerial passions and how to cope with them.

Questions for Reflection

    What role does repentance play in your understanding of communion?

    When someone says you must be "disciplined," what thoughts and feelings does this evoke? Why?

    Think of a time when you were tempted to "forsake thy cage" (your self-discipline) and run from God. What drew you back?

    What passions are you currently struggling with?

    What do you hear God calling you to do?

Redemption

Having been tenant long to a rich Lord,
    Not thriving, I resolvèd to be bold,
    And make a suit unto him, to afford
A new small-rented lease, and cancel th'old.
In heaven at his manor I him sought;   5
    They told me there, that he was lately gone
    About some land, which he had dearly bought
Long since on earth, to take possession.
I straight return'd and, knowing his great birth,
    Sought him accordingly in great resorts;   10
    In cities, theatres, gardens, parks, and courts;

> At length I heard a ragged noise and mirth
>> Of thieves and murderers—there I him espied,
>> Who straight, "Your suit is granted," said, and died.

The Poetry

This sonnet exemplifies a device often used by poets in the early seventeenth century—the *metaphysical conceit,* which is a sustained and often ingeniously unexpected metaphor. In "Redemption," the conceit involves a tenant's search for his landlord in order to present him with a petition. The tenant first seeks the landlord at his heavenly manor, only to be told that the landlord has gone to the earth. There, after vainly searching in places of pleasure, the tenant finds the landlord at Calvary. With his dying words, the landlord—even before being asked—assures the tenant that his request is granted.

The poem equates Christ's redeeming humankind by his death on the cross with a business contract. This is reflected in such terms as "tenant," "suit," and "small-rented lease," and in lines 6–8. Though the Lord is "rich," the fulfillment of his covenant, established "long since," is bought "dearly" with his love and life.

The sonnet is primarily in Shakespearean form, which consists of three quatrains, each with alternating rhyme, followed by a rhyming couplet. However, in this case the third quatrain rhymes *effe,* and the couplet is not self-contained grammatically. Herbert often experiments with form.

The Piety

The speaker in this sonnet represents the voice of God's people who seek a new or renewed relationship with God in the form of a new covenant. This is clear from the fact that the speaker has long been a tenant of the landlord, who throughout the sonnet is Christ, not God the Father. The expression "small-rented" is somewhat tongue in cheek. On the one hand, Herbert says it cost Christ dearly—indeed, his very life—to procure this new "land." On the other hand, as a free gift of God's grace, it cost the speaker nothing.

As we have seen in "The Collar," Herbert often concludes his poems with a word from the Lord. Indeed, in his best poems the word of the Lord resolves the tension. Christ is not only the Word; he has the last word in human affairs.

This sonnet draws on several important Gospel texts and ideas. In particular, it echoes the parable of the vineyard found in Mark 12:1–12. The tenants in Mark's Gospel are wicked and kill the son of the landlord when he comes to claim his due. Poem and text share a common metaphorical base that includes the death of the one to whom the property belongs.

There is intended irony throughout the poem. God, in the person of Christ, comes to earth to reclaim what belongs to him. Yet he must buy it again and at a dear price. Wisely, Herbert leaves out any speculation about the medieval idea of a ransom to Satan, focusing instead on the positive results of Christ's death. It is also ironic that the Lord of the universe is found in low estate rather than in the heavenly mansion. Indeed, he is counted among the condemned of the earth, as if he owed rather than owned society. Herbert, then, emphasizes that Christ did not come to meet our expectations but to meet our needs.

Questions for Reflection

Where would you expect a wealthy real estate developer to work and live? Where would Jesus likely reside if he walked the earth in the twenty-first century?

What is your understanding of the Old and New Covenants that Herbert alludes to with the metaphor of a business contract?

Meditate on the idea of Christ's ownership of you. What implications does this have for your life?

What areas of your life have you, the tenant, refused to give over to your Lord?

Meditate on the price Christ paid for you. Ask him to help you turn all areas of your life over to him.

Easter-Wings

Lord, who createdst man in wealth and store,
Though foolishly he lost the same,
Decaying more and more,
Till he became
Most poor: 5
With thee
O let me rise
As larks, harmoniously,
And sing this day thy victories:
Then shall the fall further the flight in me.   10

My tender age in sorrow did begin:
And still with sicknesses and shame
Thou didst so punish sin,
That I became
Most thin.   15
With thee
Let me combine,
And feel this day thy victor:
For, if I imp my wing on thine,
Affliction shall advance the flight in me.   20

The Poetry

This poem was printed on its side when it was first published in 1633. This arrangement brings out the visual message that the poem's shape conveys, and it reinforces the meaning of the words. The poem thus becomes what was then called an *emblem*. The shape can be interpreted as wings, and twice it depicts a falling and rising pattern, both concepts integral to the topic of Christ's death and resurrection.

The first stanza refers to humankind's loss of Eden and subsequent deterioration to the lowest level ("most poor"). The speaker beseeches God to let him rise and "harmoniously . . . sing," an appropriate metaphor for the poet's work. While alluding to the doctrine of the fortunate fall, the last line wittily alliterates the letter *f*.

The second stanza follows a similar pattern, as the poet deplores his own condition that has dwindled to being "most thin." But if he follows Christ's example and attaches himself to the risen Lord ("imp" means to graft feathers onto a bird's wing), he will soar out of sorrow. The letter *f* is repeated in the last line, further demonstrating Herbert's skill in combining verbal and visual effects.

The Piety

Herbert lived in an age when a good deal of the audience was familiar with the major biblical stories and the concepts of creation, fall, and redemption. In the first half of the first stanza, Herbert assumes his readers will know that after the fall the length of human life gradually diminished, as the genealogical lists in Genesis 5 attest. If the greatest wealth is a long and healthy life, then the greatest poverty is death.

The concept of *felix culpa* or the fortunate fall is indeed drawn on in the last line of the first stanza. If the fall had not happened, Christ would not have come. There would be no need for redemption or resurrection from the dead. Accordingly, the fall makes possible the recreation of humankind in the image of the resurrected one. This entire concept raises the question of whether sorrow, suffering, and death should always be seen as evil or rather as part of some greater good. At the very least, we must say that suffering and even death are things that in God's hand can be used for good (see Rom. 8:28).

Herbert, in accord with orthodox Christianity, believes that human beings are born as fallen creatures. Interestingly, in the second stanza, he puts forth the idea that God uses sickness and shame to punish sin, even in the lives of believers. Herbert holds that God is sovereign and that even occasional illnesses do not happen to believers by chance. In Herbert's case, illness made him better instead of bitter, and he begs that he might be joined more closely to Christ and so experience resurrection. He desires to be grafted into Christ and to bear his image, now spiritually but later in the flesh at the last resurrection. It is probable that some of the imagery in this poem is drawn from Malachi 4:2, which states, "But for you who revere my name the sun of righteousness shall rise, with healing in its wings. You shall go out leaping like calves from the stall." In the last half of each stanza, the believer is portrayed in the posture of a supplicant praying for spiritual and physical renewal. Resurrection is, after all, something that God alone can provide to Jesus and his followers.

Thus, Easter is not about human self-help programs but reliance on the God who raises the dead.

Questions for Reflection

In what ways have you become "most poor" in your lifetime?

How have you been able to see God's redemptive work in these situations?

What does it mean to be grafted into Christ, to bear his image?

When you suffer affliction, are you more likely to try and go it alone or to "imp" your "wing on thine"?

Take time now to ask God to use your afflictions to "further the flight" in you.

Love

Love bade me welcome; yet my soul drew back,
    Guilty of dust and sin.
But quick-ey'd Love, observing me grow slack
    From my first entrance in,
Drew nearer to me, sweetly questioning   5
    If I lack'd any thing.

"A guest," I answer'd, "worthy to be here."
    Love said, "You shall be he."
"I the unkind, ungrateful? Ah my dear,
    I cannot look on thee."   10
Love took my hand, and smiling did reply,
    "Who made the eyes but I?"

"Truth Lord, but I have marr'd them; let my shame
    Go where it doth deserve."
"And know you not," says Love, "who bore the blame?"   15
    "My dear, then I will serve."
"You must sit down," says Love, "and taste my meat."
    So I did sit and eat.

The Poetry

In these three stanzas, George Herbert creates a debate with a quietly dramatic conclusion. He cleverly modifies the erotic scenario of a potential lover coming to a feast but being inhibited from participating because of an acute sense of unworthiness. The host, personified Love, succeeds in persuading the reluctant guest to partake. Notable is the way in which Herbert characterizes Love by actions and minimizes descriptive epithets to "quick-ey'd," "sweetly," and "smiling." Moreover, Love speaks with simple directness (lines 6, 8, 12, 15, and 17) while also punning on "eye" and "I" in line 12, a witty device that Herbert's audience would have approved. Also notable is the *ababcc* rhyming pattern and the alternating of long and short lines which prevent the reader from simply treating the poem as if it had a single monotonous cadence or a rudimentary alternating rhyming pattern. The guest's reluctance is finally overcome in line 15 when reminded that Love is the guest's redeemer. The guest then gratefully agrees, "I will serve." This declaration not only reverses Lucifer's refusal to serve in heaven but also proclaims Herbert's acceptance of his role as an Anglican priest (see above on "The Collar"). He is therefore able to participate in Love's feast and will subsequently administer Holy Communion.

The Piety

At its heart, this beautiful poem focuses on the feelings of unworthiness Christians—indeed, even ministers—may feel when presented with the opportunity to partake of the body and blood of Jesus Christ, Love incarnate. While these feelings are entirely understandable, they have been grounded in a particular interpretation of Paul's admonition in 1 Corinthians 11:27–30: "Whoever, therefore, eats the bread or drinks the cup of the Lord in an unworthy manner will be answerable for the body and blood of the Lord. Examine yourselves, and only then eat of the bread and drink of the cup. For all who eat and drink without discerning the body, eat and drink judgment against themselves." Notice, however, Paul is not speaking of being worthy to partake of communion but of partaking in a worthy or appropriate manner. Strictly speaking, since we all are sinners who fall short of God's best, no one could ever be worthy of partaking of the Eucharist. Worthiness is not the issue. Indeed, feelings of repentance and remorse for sin are quite in order as we prepare for communion. In the poem, the speaker is going through this period of self-examination and quite rightly feels unworthy.

One must bear in mind that these feelings were likely to be acute if one grew up in the Catholic tradition, which affirmed that the Eucharist became the actual body and blood of Christ by means of transubstantiation in the celebration of the Mass, or if one adhered to the Anglican notion of the real spiritual presence of Christ in the elements. In either case, the communicant would believe he or she was not merely encountering Love but actually partaking of Love in the feast.

Notice in the poem that Love's answer to the soul's dilemma is twofold. In stanza two, Love appeals to its work as the creator, but this answer does not prove to be decisive. In stanza three, Love alludes to Christ's death on the cross—he bore the blame and erased the need for standing back or being ashamed. This latter answer finally convinces the speaker to act.

The conclusion is also striking, for Herbert speaks of serving by participating in the feast. He puts forth the idea of presenting ourselves to God as our service or true worship, in this case by means of partaking in the liturgy (see Rom. 12:1). It is intriguing that the word *liturgy* comes to us from the Greek *leitourgia*, which literally means public service, ministry, or worship. Herbert likely intends a double entendre here, especially as the context is a discussion of partaking of communion. He will worship by partaking of the service; he will serve by joining the feast; and he will minister (serve) by partaking of and celebrating the Eucharist. In other words, Herbert reaffirms his call to ministry by taking up one of the chief ministerial liturgies or services.

In the end, there is also a certain eschatological aspect to this poem. Jesus depicted the consummation of God's kingdom on earth as a banquet where we will sit down to feast with the returning king (Matt. 26:29). Significantly, the poem's Love imagery comports with texts that suggest the eschatological banquet will be a wedding feast between Christ and his church (Matt. 22:1–14; 25:1–13; Luke 12:35–40). Like the speaker in the poem, human beings can only be invited guests at such a banquet. We may attend because of the graciousness of the host, not because we have earned or deserve a place at the table.

Questions for Reflection

What "dust and sin" exist in your life that make you draw back from God?

Reflect on the idea that God made your eyes and every other part of you. What does this say about the nature of God?

Does the image of God as a wooing lover challenge your perception of God? What does this image say about God's character?

Meditate on the idea of the kingdom of God as a banquet feast. What images does this bring to mind? What emotions? What does the image of a feast say about the nature of God's coming kingdom?

How is participation in communion a matter of serving? Why does God desire for us to take part in communion? How does Christ's death allow you to come to the table?

Take a few moments to praise God for the attributes you named above and to thank God for his desire to include you in the wedding feast.

FIVE

Andrew Marvell
(1621–78)

Born in Yorkshire, Marvell attended Hull Grammar School, then went to Trinity College, Cambridge from 1633–39. He contributed Latin and Greek verses to a 1637 volume congratulating Charles I on the birth of his daughter. After his father drowned in 1641, Marvell moved to London, then spent 1643–47 traveling in Holland, France, Spain, and Italy. In 1648–49 he wrote poems about his Royalist friends, but in 1650 he composed a Horatian ode celebrating the victories of Oliver Cromwell. This he followed with poems commemorating the marriage of Cromwell's daughter and Cromwell's death in 1658. Marvell also served as tutor to the daughter of Parliamentary General Thomas Fairfax from 1650–52 and later as tutor to a ward of Cromwell's. In 1657 Marvell succeeded John Milton as Latin Secretary to the Council of State. In 1659 he was elected a member of Parliament for his hometown of Hull, a position he retained until his death. He was known for frequently attacking corruption in Parliament and at court. Marvell also wrote prose against the growing Catholic influence in the Stuart court and in favor of toleration for Protestant Nonconformists. His *Miscellaneous Poems* (not including his political satires) were published posthumously in 1681.

On a Drop of Dew

See how the orient dew,
Shed from the bosom of the morn

    Into the blowing roses,
Yet careless of its mansion new,
For the clear region where 'twas born   5
    Round in itself incloses,
    And in its little globe's extent
Frames as it can its native element;
    How it the purple flow'r does slight,
    Scarce touching where it lies,   10
But gazing back upon the skies,
    Shines with a mournful light
    Like its own tear,
Because so long divided from the sphere.
    Restless it rolls and unsecure,   15
    Trembling lest it grow impure,
    Till the warm sun pity its pain,
And to the skies exhale it back again.
    So the soul, that drop, that ray
Of the clear fountain of eternal day,   20
Could it within the human flower be seen,
    Rememb'ring still its former height,
    Shuns the sweet leaves and blossoms green;
    And recollecting its own light,
Does, in its pure and circling thoughts, express   25
The greater heaven in an heaven less.
    In how coy a figure wound,
    Every way it turns away;
    So the world excluding round,
    Yet receiving in the day;   30
    Dark beneath but bright above,
    Here disdaining, there in love;
How loose and easy hence to go,
How girt and ready to ascend,
Moving but on a point below,   35
It all about does upwards bend
Such did the manna's sacred dew distill,
White and entire, though congealed and chill,
Congealed on earth: but does, dissolving, run
Into the glories of the almighty sun.   40

The Poetry

Like Herbert's "Redemption," this poem involves a metaphysical conceit, in this case comparing a drop of dew to the human

soul. Both have fallen from heaven, and both yearn to return there.

The first eighteen lines give a vivid picture of a dewdrop. A product of the morning, it incorporates within its circular shape a heavenly light that outshines the color of the flower on which it rolls. Marvell endows nature with feelings. The dewdrop is reluctant to be on earth (lines 4 and 10–17), where it fears becoming corrupted. Recognizing its plight, the sun evaporates it so that it can return to heaven.

The turn from the natural object to the soul is announced at line 19. The soul is described as having the same characteristics as the drop of dew, with emphasis on the soul's awareness of originating in the light of heaven, its eagerness to return there, and its affinity with heaven (expressed in the microcosm-macrocosm analogy of lines 24–26). The last two couplets relate the drop of dew to manna, the white, sweet food God miraculously provided to the Hebrews during their forty-year sojourn in the desert. Whether by intention or coincidence, the poem is forty lines long.

The Piety

During the medieval period of church history, Platonism became the dominant hermeneutic used to interpret the spiritual. In particular, it affected how people evaluated the spiritual and material realms. The latter was seen as a pale, transient, and corruptible copy of the former. This way of thinking affected the theology of the human soul, and the discussion centered on the idea of a well of souls in heaven. The soul was believed to be inherently immortal, existing in heaven before ever being temporarily joined to a human body and longing to return to that perfect world. This is the theology that undergirds Marvell's poem. It is a very different theology of spiritual nature than the one we find in the New Testament. In the New Testament, there is no inherently immortal soul. Human beings, in both body and soul, have finite beginnings. Everlasting life is possible only in salvation through faith in Christ.

Nevertheless, something in this poem strikes at the heart of Christian piety, and that is a longing for perfection, a sighing for Eden or heaven. The New Testament vision of how and when this will transpire focuses not on dying and going to heaven, but on the ultimate merger of heaven and earth as described in Revelation 21. There a picture is given of heaven coming down and earth being transformed, including its human inhabitants by means of resurrection. Resurrection, not the immortality of the soul, is what Christians should long for, as it involves the redemption of the whole person. Even manna from heaven cannot compare to when God's realm will once again invade our realm and "glory fills our souls."

Questions for Reflection

When you think of eternity, how do you view the afterlife?

What do you think of when you hear the term *soul?*

Take time to assess what things you really long for in life, and probe whether these things match up with the New Testament visions for the future.

SIX

Henry Vaughan
(1621–95)

Henry Vaughan and his twin brother Thomas were born in New-ton by the River Usk in the county of Breconshire, Wales. By 1638, they were apparently at Jesus College, Oxford, but by 1640 Henry moved to London to study law. After the outbreak of civil war in 1642, he returned to Wales and may have seen military service on the Royalist side. His *Poems* (1646) and *Olor Iscanus* (*The Swan of Usk* [1651]) are largely secular and in the fashion of the school of Ben Jonson. But following his immersion in the poetry of George Herbert, religion became the dominant theme in Vaughan's poetry. The death of his younger brother William and the defeat of the Royalist cause may have also contributed. In any case, Vaughan's *Silex Scintillans* (*The Sparkling Flint* [1650; enlarged 1655]) is one of the century's most distinctive collections of religious poetry. He later wrote several prose translations of devotional works and spent the last four decades of his life as a physician in his native Breconshire.

Religion

My God, when I walk in those groves
And leaves thy spirit still doth fan,
I see in each shade that there grows
An angel talking with a man.

Under a juniper some house,   5
Or the cool myrtle's canopy,
Others beneath an oak's green boughs,
Or at some fountain's bubbling eye;

Here Jacob dreams and wrestles; there
Elias by a raven is fed,   10
Another time by the angel, where
He brings him water with his bread;

In Abraham's tent the wingèd guests
(O how familiar then was heaven!)
Eat, drink, discourse, sit down, and rest   15
Until the cool and shady even;

Nay, thou thyself, my God, in fire,
Whirlwinds, and clouds, and the soft voice
Speak'st there so much, that I admire
We have no conference in these days.   20

Is the truce broke? or 'cause we have
A mediator now with thee,
Dost thou therefore old treaties waive
And by appeals from him decree?

Or is't so, as some green heads say,   25
That now all miracles must cease,
Though thou hast promised they should stay
The tokens of the Church, and peace?

No, no; religion is a spring
That from some secret, golden mine   30
Derives her birth, and thence doth bring
Cordials in every drop, and wine;

But in her long and hidden course
Passing through the earth's dark veins,
Grows still from better unto worse,   35
And both her taste and colour stains,

Then drilling on, learns to increase
False echoes, and confusèd sounds,
And unawares doth often seize
On veins of sulphur underground;   40

So poisoned, breaks forth in some clime,
And at first sight doth many please,

But drunk, is puddle, or mere slime
And 'stead of physic, a disease.

Just such a tainted sink we have   45
Like that Samaritan's dead well,
Nor must we for the kernel crave
Because most voices like the shell.

Heal then these waters, Lord; or bring thy flock,
Since these are troubled, to the springing rock.   50
Look down, great Master of the Feast! O shine,
And turn once more our water into wine!

The Poetry

Like many religious poems of the seventeenth century, "Religion" abounds in biblical references that Vaughan could confidently expect his audience to recognize. The poem creates a sense that the speaker is engaged in an intimate dialogue with God. This is seen in the first quatrain and in the questions that begin in line 19, where Vaughan "admire[s]" (i.e., is surprised) that in his era God and human beings are no longer conversing. It is also suggested by lines 23–28, where those who declare that the age of miracles is past are dismissed as "green heads." Vaughan frequently uses onomatopoeia, as seen in the second quatrain, in the change to "soft voice" at the end of line 17, and in lines 43–44.

Particularly striking is the expansion of the last quatrain from lines of eight syllables to ten. This lends emphasis to the concluding prayer, the last line of which combines explicit reference to the miracle at the wedding feast in Cana with hints of the Eucharist.

The Piety

In this remarkable poem, Henry Vaughan offers us a comparison of religion in his own day and in ages past. He characterizes his age as being unlike the Old Testament era when there was intimate, face-to-face contact with the Almighty and when miracles abounded. Indeed, in the first stanza, he characterizes biblical antiquity as a time when an angel was conversing with a human under each tree. By contrast, Vaughan says he is surprised that "we have no conference in these days" (line 20).

Yet in line 30, Vaughan protests against those who say the age of miracles has long passed away. The problem, he says, is that true religion is like a spring that has traveled far over the centuries. Not surprisingly, the water has become tainted along the way so that believers drink from a dead well (line 46). People have grown accustomed to the taste, but it is causing sickness rather than health (line 44). The solution, then, is not to settle for religion that is less than pure, but to request a new miracle, where God once more leads his flock to a pure, clear spring or turns tainted water into life-giving wine.

The poem has a cornucopia of biblical images and terms (e.g., juniper [1 Kings 19:5]; myrtle [Zech. 1:8–11]; oak [Judg. 6:11]; fountain [Gen. 16:7]; fire [Exod. 3:2]; whirlwind [Job 38:1]; well [John 4:5–15]; rock [Exod. 17:6]; Cana [John 2:1–10]). The overarching image is that of the pilgrim's regress from a verdant garden to a land that is dry and weary and has only tainted wells. Vaughan then addresses the spiritual and pastoral problem of what to do when so far removed from earlier times of blessing and intimacy with God. Do we accept the state of barrenness, the dark night of the soul, and make a virtue of what seems a necessity? Or do we beseech God to once again perform miracles? Vaughan's answer is stated plainly in the last stanza. The God of ages past is the God of the present and may still be sought for healing and help and miracles. It is not necessary to return to a halcyon age to experience such a blessed state. It was not the age that provided the help or the locale that offered succor but the God who was found in those times and places.

Questions for Reflection

What "veins of sulphur" today pollute true religion?

What do you think true, unpolluted religion consists of?

What miracles have you experienced in your life or seen in the lives of others around you?

What are your "conferences" with God like? How would you like to see them change? What can you do to improve your conferences with God?

Read John 2:1–11. Take a few minutes to reflect on how God takes the ordinary and transforms it into the extraordinary. Ask God to transform your spiritual walk with him.

The Retreat

Happy those early days! when I
Shined in my angel-infancy.
Before I understood this place
Appointed for my second race,
Or taught my soul to fancy ought   5
But a white, celestial thought,
When yet I had not walked above
A mile or two, from my first love,
And looking back (at that short space)
Could see a glimpse of his bright face;   10
When on some *gilded cloud,* or *flower*
My gazing soul would dwell an hour,
And in those weaker glories spy
Some shadows of eternity;
Before I taught my tongue to wound   15
My conscience with a sinful sound,
Or had the black art to dispense
A sev'ral sin to ev'ry sense,
But felt through all this fleshly dress
Bright *shoots* of everlastingness.   20
   O how I long to travel back
And tread again that ancient track!
That I might once more reach that plain,
Where first I left my glorious train,
From whence th' inlightened spirit sees   25
That shady city of palm trees;
But (ah!) my soul with too much stay
Is drunk, and staggers in the way.
Some men a forward motion love,
But I by backward steps would move,   30
And when this dust falls to the urn
In that state I came return.

The Poetry

   The title can mean either moving backwards or withdrawing
from the world for religious concentration. The opening lines
link the ideal of childlike innocence as expressed by Jesus with
the Platonic concept of the soul's preexistence. Hence, earthly
existence is a "second race" in which sin increasingly darkens us
(line 4). The speaker longs "to travel back" (line 21) to a condi-

tion of enlightenment akin to Moses' vision of Jericho, the "city of palm trees" (line 26).

Throughout the poem, the imagery of light and brightness signifies the eternal divine. Natural objects such as the "gilded cloud or flower" are "weaker glories" through which we "spy / Some shadows of eternity" (lines 11–14). This accords with Plato's theory that the material world is an inadequate copy of an ideal universe, an idea easily equatable with the Christian concept of heaven. Vaughan again incorporates a Platonic idea in lines 27–28: "But (ah!) my soul with too much stay / Is drunk, and staggers in the way." In Plato's *Phaedo*, Socrates asks, "Were we not saying that the soul is dragged by the body into the region of the changeable, wanders, and is confused; the world spins around her, she is like a drunkard when she touches change? But when returning into herself she reflects, she passes into the other world, the region of purity and eternity and immortality and unchangeableness, which are her kindred" (Jowett's translation). Vaughan concludes by wishing that at his death he will return to the state of childhood innocence in which he entered life.

The Piety

Like several of the Romantic poets (e.g., Wordsworth and Coleridge) who offered "intimations of immortality" and spoke of the human soul coming into this world "trailing clouds of glory," Vaughan offers a reverie on what his former life in heaven must have been like. He longs to go back to that condition. Absent once again is any reflection on the fact that the New Testament stresses looking forward, not backward, to everlasting life. Our hope should be resurrection from the dead rather than disembodied bliss in heaven.

Nevertheless, this poem offers a good opportunity to reflect on what heaven is like. Is it merely a perfected form of earthly existence, like a beautiful spring day in the mountains without any flies? Or is heaven a different state altogether, where there is not merely the absence of suffering, sorrow, disease, decay, and death but the presence of all that is good, true, and beautiful? Is heaven merely a haven from all that is dark and dangerous, or is it the place where life's yes is truly much more powerful than death's no? Whatever else we may wish to say about heaven, it is truly a place where there is no sin or evil, for it is the dwelling place of a holy God. In this respect, it is rightly seen as a place where there is no shadow of turning and no darkness.

Yet Vaughan, like the later Romantics, also seems to confuse the issues of innocence and holiness when it comes to the early stages of human life. When we speak of a child being innocent, we presume the child has committed no willful sin and thus lacks experience of trespasses. This is not the same thing as holiness. The absence of the experience of evil is not the same as the presence of good. Therefore, saying a child is innocent is not the same as saying the child is pure or good. An adequate theology of human fallenness prevents us from idealizing human infancy as the most desirable state. At the same time, Vaughan expresses a frequent desire of all Christians who long for the simpler, less complicated, less sinful times of youth.

Questions for Reflection

Are you more likely to look forward to what lies ahead in your life or to look back at what is already past? Why?

Which do you need more of in your Christian walk—the absence of evil or the presence of good?

Do you believe, like Vaughan, that your soul existed in heaven before your birth? Why or why not?

What do you imagine bodily resurrection will be like?

What do you most hope will be a part of heaven and the resurrection?

The Waterfall

With what deep murmurs through time's silent stealth
Doth thy transparent, cool and watery wealth
    Here flowing fall,
    And chide, and call,
As if his liquid, loose retinue stayed   5
Lingering, and were of this steep place afraid,
    The common pass
    Where, clear as glass,
    All must descend
    Not to an end: 10

But quickened by this deep and rocky grave,
Rise to a longer course more bright and brave.
Dear stream! dear bank, where often I
Have sat, and pleased my pensive eye,
Why, since each drop of thy quick store   15
Runs thither, whence it flowed before,
Should poor souls fear a shade or night,
Who came (sure) from a sea of light?
Or since those drops are all sent back
So sure to thee, that none doth lack,   20
Why should frail flesh doubt any more
That what God takes, he'll not restore?
O useful element and clear!
My sacred wash and cleanser here,
My first consigner unto those   25
Fountains of life, where the Lamb goes!
What sublime truths, and wholesome themes,
Lodge in thy mystical, deep streams!
Such as dull man can never find
Unless that Spirit lead his mind,   30
Which first upon thy face did move,
And hatched all with his quickening love.
As this loud brook's incessant fall
In streaming rings restagnates all,
Which reach by course the bank, and then   35
Are no more seen, just so pass men.
O my invisible estate,
My glorious liberty, still late!
Thou art the channel my soul seeks,
Not this with cataracts and creeks.   40

The Poetry

Vaughan presents the waterfall as both a natural object and a symbol. In the first twelve lines, he employs onomatopoeia extensively to convey the sense of water flowing quietly to the brink and then cascading precipitously down. This process is compared to the quiet passage of time that carries us with "silent stealth" (line 1) toward death, that "steep place" of which we are afraid (line 6). Paradoxically, through that fall we are "quickened" (line 11). Not only are we made to move faster, but we are also brought to life (as in the Prayer Book's references to "the quick and the dead"). This meaning is repeated in "quick store" (line 15) and "quickening" (line 32).

Lines 15–22 question why we should be afraid, since we are of divine origin. Like water recycling to its source, our souls will return to heaven, that "sea of light." In lines 24–26, the life-giving quality of water is transmuted into the sacrament of baptism, which is first "consigner" or deliverer of Vaughan into the presence of Christ. This emphasis on the symbolic power of water is extended in lines 30–32 with an invocation of the creation story in Genesis. The word "restagnates" (line 34) in Vaughan's lifetime usually meant "overflows." The concluding four lines make plain that he seeks to transcend the worldly reality of the waterfall in favor of the heavenly "channel."

The Piety

The imagery of "The Waterfall" must not be mistaken for the pagan notion of death as a journey across the River Styx into the netherworld. Here water represents life, which must come to a point of descent into a "rocky grave" (line 11) only to rise again. The soul is like water that must pass through various channels in life. In the last two lines, Vaughan suggests that he has a choice in his life passages.

Missing entirely from this poem is the idea of death as an enemy or a penalty for sin. Rather, in lines 17–18 the poet emphasizes that death should not be feared. It is part of life's natural process and ultimately comes from the hand of God. Furthermore, Vaughan assumes the eternality of the soul. The soul has come from God and returns to him. The New Testament says nothing of this latter idea. On the contrary, the Bible emphasizes that we are dust and that we return to dust unless given the special gift of eternal life. The piety Vaughan reflects is typical of the church after the early Middle Ages, when it had been heavily influenced by Platonic thought about the soul. Some of the essentially Jewish beliefs about the origin of life, the nature of death, and the resurrection had been displaced or reinterpreted by Greek philosophies like the eternality of the soul.

Thus, this poem gives readers an excellent opportunity to reflect on what they really believe about the nature of life, death, and the afterlife. Is there a heavenly well where all souls exist prior to being united with bodies on earth? Is there a point in time before which each individual creature did not exist, either on earth or in heaven? Is life inherently everlasting, or is everlasting life a gift that only some receive through Christ, the "channel"? As Vaughan suggests, the answers to such questions "dull man can never find / Unless that Spirit lead his mind" (lines 29–30).

Questions for Reflection

If God were to reveal one thing to you about death or the afterlife, what would you ask him?

Meditate on the idea of water and the many forms it takes. How many symbols of the Christian faith speak to you in these images?

"Through the fall we are . . . brought to life." What falls has God used in your life to bring you renewal?

What fears are you facing right now?

Take a few minutes to ask God for his peace and wisdom to address these fears.

They Are All Gone into the World of Light!

They are all gone into the world of light!
    And I alone sit ling'ring here;
Their very memory is fair and bright,
    And my sad thoughts doth clear.

It glows and glitters in my cloudy breast   5
    Like stars upon some gloomy grove,
Or those faint beams in which this hill is dressed,
    After the sun's remove.

I see them walking in an air of glory,
    Whose light doth trample on my days: 10
My days, which are at best but dull and hoary,
    Mere glimmering and decays.

O holy hope! and high humility,
    High as the Heavens above!
These are your walks, and you have showed them me   15
    To kindle my cold love,

> Dear, beauteous death! the jewel of the just,
>   Shining nowhere, but in the dark;
> What mysteries do lie beyond thy dust;
>   Could man outlook that mark!   20
>
> He that hath found some fledged bird's nest may know
>   At first sight, if the bird be flown;
> But what fair well, or grove he sings in now,
>   That is to him unknown.
>
> And yet, as angels in some brighter dreams   25
>   Call to the soul, when man doth sleep:
> So some strange thoughts transcend our wonted themes,
>   And into glory peep.
>
> If a star were confined into a tomb
>   Her captive flames must needs burn there;   30
> But when the hand that locked her up gives room,
>   She'll shine through all the sphere.
>
> O Father of eternal life, and all
>   Created glories under thee!
> Resume thy spirit from this world of thrall   35
>   Into true liberty.
>
> Either disperse these mists, which blot and fill
>   My perspective (still) as they pass,
> Or else remove me hence unto that hill,
>   Where I shall need no glass.   40

The Poetry

This is one of Vaughan's untitled poems. "They" refers to his
dead friends and perhaps to his younger brother William and his
first wife Elizabeth. Characteristically, Vaughan imagines them
in heaven, "the world of light." His memory of them illuminates
("doth clear") his "sad thoughts," as stars or the sun's last beams
counteract darkness. The alliteration of lines 13–14 emphasizes
his eagerness to look beyond the fact that the body will be re-
duced to dust.

In the fifth quatrain, death is addressed in rapturous language
as the gateway to light. The next three quatrains present images

of flight or escape. These lead to the prayer in the last two quatrains in which the Father-creator is asked to take back and lib-
erate the speaker's soul from this world and to either dispel the
darkness or carry him to heaven so that he will no longer need
to view it from afar as through a telescope ("perspective" and
"glass").

The Piety

This poem is full of what we have all experienced at one time
or another—world weariness. The older we get, and the more
we see our friends and relatives pass away, the more alone we
feel. Couple this with the health battles we experience as we get
older, and it is no surprise that from time to time we look with
longing or envy on the state of the those who have gone to
heaven before us.

When we experience such struggles and the resulting battles
with depression, we may find some solace and wisdom in the
conclusion of this poem. Notice how Vaughan does the right
thing with such despairing or troubling thoughts—he prays
and leaves his reflections in God's hands. Notice also that
Vaughan asks for one of two things. On the one hand, he asks
for a clearer vision and perspective on life so that he may see it
as God sees it. On the other hand, he asks to be allowed to go
on to heaven itself, where "one will see face to face." Some
Christians think it is wrong to express these sorts of thoughts.
We are supposed to be stoic and never complain or admit we
are tired of this life, for it may sound too much like ingratitude.
Yet, I am struck by how much this poem has the same tone as
some of the psalms, particularly the laments. The lesson to be
learned from reading the psalms, as from reading this poem, is
that we must be honest with God and with ourselves. Whatever
our cares and concerns, we should take them to the Lord in
prayer. This Vaughan does, and he leaves the outcome of his requests in God's hands. In this, he provides us all with an example to follow in times of struggle.

Questions for Reflection

Take a few moments to recall fond memories of loved ones who have
passed away. Thank God for the joy they have brought to your life.

What feelings does "Dear, beauteous death! the jewel of the just" evoke? Have you ever thought of death in this way? Why or why not?

When have you experienced the most "world weariness"?

Take time now to bring your complaints before God in your own lament. Ask for God's perspective, and ask him to help you leave these complaints in his hands.

The World

1

I saw Eternity the other night
Like a great *Ring* of pure and endless light,
    All calm, as it was bright,
And round beneath it, Time in hours, days, years
    Driven by the spheres   5
Like a vast shadow moved, in which the world
    And all her train were hurled;
The doting lover in his quaintest strain
    Did there complain,
Near him, his lute, his fancy, and his flights,   10
    Wit's sour delights,
With gloves, and knots the silly snares of pleasure
    Yet his dear treasure
All scattered lay, while he his eyes did pour
    Upon a flower.   15

2

The darksome states-man hung with weights and woe
Like a thick midnight-fog moved there so slow
    He did nor stay, nor go;
Condemning thoughts (like sad eclipses) scowl
    Upon his soul,   20
And clouds of crying witnesses without
    Pursued him with one shout.
Yet digged the mole, and lest his ways be found
    Worked under ground,
Where he did clutch his prey, but one did see   25
    That policy,
Churches and altars fed him, perjuries
    Were gnats and flies,

It rained about him blood and tears, but he
    Drank them as free.   30

3

The fearful miser on a heap of rust
Sat pining all his life there, did scarce trust
    His own hands with the dust,
Yet would not place one piece above, but lives
    In fear of thieves.   35
Thousands there were as frantic as himself
    And hugged each one his pelf,
The down-right epicure placed heaven in sense
    And scorned pretence
While others slipped into a wide excess   40
    Said little less;
The weaker sort slight, trivial wares enslave
    Who think them brave,
And poor, despised truth sat counting by
    Their victory.   45

4

Yet some, who all this while did weep and sing,
And sing, and weep, soared up into the *Ring*,
    But most would use no wing.
O fools (said I,) thus to prefer dark night
    Before true light,   50
To live in grots, and caves, and hate the day
    Because it shows the way,
The way which from this dead and dark abode
    Leads up to God,
A way where you might tread the Sun, and be   55
    More bright than he.
But as I did their madness so discuss
    One whispered thus,
This ring the bride-groom did for none provide
    But for his bride.   60

1 John 2:16–17
All that is in the world, the lust of the flesh, and the lust of the eyes,
and the pride of life, is not of the Father, but is of the world. And the
world passeth away, and the lusts thereof: but he that doeth the will
of God abideth for ever. (KJV)

The Poetry

Vaughan vividly depicts the world as a place where most of its inhabitants (the "train" of line 7) waste their lives in futile or destructive pursuits. He reinforces that view by the appended quotation from 1 John.

The lover is depicted in ambiguous terms. He is "doting." He "complains" (a common term for uttering love sentiments that go unrequited) in "quaintest strains" (i.e., elaborate flights of fancy). Love tokens are carelessly strewn around him while he pours tears (or pores) over a flower. Ironically, the statesman is a dark and sinister figure whose apparent immobility hides his destructive underground maneuvers. This figure may owe something to Vaughan's sympathy for King Charles I, who was executed in 1649 by Oliver Cromwell's Roundhead party. Several kinds of materialists are denounced: the miser who will not invest in anything heavenly ("would not place one piece above"); self-indulgent sensualists (lines 38–41); and those who succumb to the enticements of consumerism.

This world, however, is juxtaposed with eternity. In the opening seven lines, the calm ring of eternal light is contrasted with the time-dominated world of the ever-revolving seven spheres of Ptolemaic cosmology. This is one of the Platonic concepts Vaughan liked to employ, as is the image in the fourth stanza of humans as benighted cave dwellers. Vaughan adds to this the Christian concept of the penitent, who soars heavenward toward God and the Sun (Son). The ring then becomes the wedding ring Christ the bridegroom gives to his bride the church. The poem, intricately shaped in four stanzas containing a triplet and six couplets, is itself encircled by ring imagery.

The Piety

First John 2:16–17 is in part the text for this poetic meditation, and it stresses that lust and pride are not qualities that characterize or come from God. Rather, they characterize and come from the world. God and heaven are characterized by light while the world and its ways are characterized by darkness. This sort of limited dualism is common in Johannine literature, especially 1 John, which is quoted at the end of the poem. The poem, like the biblical literature, emphasizes that human beings love darkness more than light, our ways more than God's ways.

One of the more effective parts of "The World" is the contrast between the circle of light—the eternal circle, without beginning or end and symbolized by the wedding band—and the rat race that we find ourselves in—endless running in circles to no end. The difference between the two figures is not their shape but their purpose and direction. It is possible to live life in a symmetrical, orderly fashion and yet have no purpose. The lover, the statesman, the miser, the epicurean—all are people who, instead of ruling their passions, are ruled by their passions and tailor their behavior to serve their longings.

Yet Vaughan suggests there is one greater longing that, left unsatisfied, makes satisfying lesser needs such as love, influence, or financial security pointless. That great longing is the longing for God himself. Pascal once stated that there is a God-shaped vacuum in every human heart, which only God can fill. Yet human beings seek unsuccessfully to fill up that void with money, food, accomplishments, or human passion. The cyclical composition of this poem reminds us that, while the world and its passions are ephemeral, God and his purposes abide forever and so do those who do his will in this veil of tears where the saints both sing and weep.

Questions for Reflection

Try to remember the darkest moment in your life. What were your deepest fears and longings at that moment?

Now try to remember the brightest moment in your life. What were your greatest joys and longings on that occasion?

In what ways do you see yourself trapped in an endless cycle of activities, sometimes seemingly pointless activities?

How does Vaughan suggest breaking that cycle?

It has sometimes been said that "the good is the enemy of the best." In what ways have you found this to be true? In what ways could human pride become an obstacle to your reaching for God's highest and best for your life?

SEVEN

Isaac Watts
(1674–1748)

After being educated at King Edward VI Grammar School in Southampton and Stoke Newington Dissenting Academy, Isaac Watts became a minister. A prolific poet, his aim was "to promote the pious entertainment of souls truly serious, even of the meanest capacity." Accordingly, though he wrote some poems of considerable technical difficulty, he also cultivated simplicity in such poems as "Our God, Our Help in Ages Past" from *The Psalms of David* and "How Doth the Little Busy Bee" from *Divine Songs for the Use of Children* (which became so popular as to be parodied by Lewis Carroll).

Crucifixion to the World by the Cross of Christ
(Galatians 6:14)

When I survey the wondrous Cross
    Where the young Prince of Glory died,
My richest gain I count but loss,
    And pour contempt on all my pride.

Forbid it, Lord, that I should boast   5
    Save in the death of Christ, my God;
All the vain things that charm me most,
    I sacrifice them to his blood.

See from his head, his hands, his feet,
    Sorrow and love flow mingled down;   10
Did e'er such love and sorrow meet?
    Or thorns compose so rich a crown?

His dying crimson like a robe
   Spreads o'er his body on the Tree,
Then am I dead to all the globe,   15
   And all the globe is dead to me.

Were the whole realm of nature mine,
   That were a present far too small;
Love so amazing, so divine,
   Demands my soul, my life, my all.   20

The Poetry

This hymn owes something to the tradition of the formal meditation as defined in Catholic (mainly Jesuit) and Protestant devotional manuals of the sixteenth and seventeenth centuries and as demonstrated in poems by John Donne and others. In the meditation, the speaker first visualizes a religious scene, then analyzes its meaning and concludes in prayer.

The opening two lines of the first, third, and fourth quatrains all invoke the visual, with "survey," "see," and the image of Christ's blood streaming down his body. In each case, they are followed by contradictions: gain turns into loss, pride becomes contempt, love unites with sorrow, thorns compose a crown, the speaker becomes dead to the world. These contradictions move the speaker from calm detachment in the opening line to emotional involvement with the image and meaning of the crucifixion. Recognizing Christ's sacrifice leads the speaker to proclaim that he must reject his egocentricity and give himself entirely to Christ.

In the original title, Watts cited Galatians 6:14: "But God forbid that I should glory, save in the cross of our Lord Jesus Christ, by whom the world is crucified unto me, and I unto the world" (KJV). The first half of that text is echoed in lines 5–6 and the second half in lines 15–16. In the latter, Watts skillfully employs chiasmus, a device in which the second half of a statement is grammatically balanced against the first but with the parts inverted. Thus, the subject "I" and the object "globe" are switched so that "globe" becomes the subject and "me" becomes the object. The second line in the first edition—"Where the young Prince of Glory died"—was later changed to eliminate the inappropriate word "young." The stronger line, "On which the Prince of Glory died," was substituted. This change also helped maintain the iambic tetrameter (four pairs, each with an unstressed syllable followed by a stressed syllable).

The Piety

At the heart of this most famous of Isaac Watts's hymns is a meditation on a series of paradoxes—how loss becomes gain, how glory is manifested in something shameful, how sorrow and love can coexist, how only the shameful cross should be praised, how thorns can make a glorious crown, and how the greatest offering is too little.

In the first stanza, Watts takes up the posture of an observer of the crucifixion. But unlike those first observers (e.g., Mark 15), he sees Jesus' death through Christian eyes. Christ is already the "Prince of Glory" even before the resurrection, and the cross is already a wondrous thing. The first stanza suggests that nothing Watts has could be of the same value as Christ's death, and reflecting on that death causes the ultimate transvaluation of values. Not only does Watts's richest worldly gain seem paltry, but his human pride now seems totally ridiculous.

The theme of pride is carried over into the first line of the second stanza, and it suggests that Watts needs help with boasting and pride. God must forbid him from such human preening and from overvaluing "all the vain things that charm me most." Watts must sacrifice such vanities to Christ's blood, just as Christ sacrificed himself so that Watts might be changed. The internal change is referred to in the third stanza when Watts says he is dead to all the world, and the world is dead to him. Paradoxically, it is not as if he thinks the world is now of no value. Rather, he recognizes its immense value (see the last stanza); but that value is miniscule compared to the value of Christ's death. The poet is now dead to the enticement of the world, but he has not lost a sense of the world's worth.

Recognizing the value of Christ's death comes at a price. It represents such amazing and divine love that it demands of its beneficiary total commitment—soul, life, all that one has and is. If Christ has given all, he also demands as much. If the world has charmed the author, he has been transfixed by a higher passion in the ultimate example of self-sacrifice. And this sacrifice is not offered up by just anyone. In Watts's words, it has been offered by "Christ, my God."

In the end, these stanzas are permeated not only with a sense of wonder but with a sense of being overwhelmed that God would go so far to redeem an ordinary mortal who struggles with pride, boasting, and the enticements of the world, the flesh, and the devil. The idea that "while we were yet sinners, Christ died for us," stands behind every line of this poem and explains the wonder and awe of the poet. It is one thing to die for a good cause but quite another to die for those who have rejected you. That the God of the universe would be doing such a thing gives new meaning to the word *grace,* which by definition means undeserved benefit, unmerited favor.

Questions for Reflection

What contradictions has God brought into your life? (What gain has God turned to loss? What loss has he turned to gain? etc.)

What does it mean in your life to be "dead to all the globe" (dead to the world)?

What things in your life are you most proud of?

Which of these would you be least able to give up?

Reflect on the idea that Christ gave up everything for you. Take time to thank him for his sacrifice.

What more can you give to God that you have not already offered up to him? Pray for God's help to do this.

EIGHT

John Newton
(1725–1807)

The author of the hymn popularized under the title "Amazing Grace" had a remarkable life. John Newton went to sea at age eleven and eventually became captain of a slave ship. Converted during a dangerous storm, he entered the ministry and worked for the campaign to abolish slavery in the British Empire, a goal finally achieved in 1833.

Faith's Review and Expectation

Amazing grace! How sweet the sound
   That saved a wretch like me!
I once was lost, but now am found;
   Was blind, but now I see.

'Twas grace that taught my heart to fear,   5
   And grace my fears relieved;
How precious did that grace appear
   The hour I first believed.

Through many dangers, toils, and snares,
   I have already come;   10
'Tis grace hath brought me safe thus far,
   And grace will lead me home.

The Lord has promised good to me,
   His word my hope secures;
He will my shield and portion be,   15
   As long as life endures.

The Poetry

In this hymn, "grace" is the dominant word, appearing six times in the first three quatrains. Its saving effects are seen in the pairs "lost" and "found," "blind" and "see," "fear" and "fears relieved," "safe" and "home." Reviewing his past (quatrains one and two) and present (quatrain three), the speaker can look to the future with confidence (quatrain four). Although the use of first-person pronouns throughout may suggest egocentricity, it equally conveys a sense of intense personal experience. The popularity of this hymn in the later twentieth century demonstrates its wide appeal.

The Piety

The danger in dealing with this hymn is that it has become so familiar we hardly hear what it is saying. The same may be said about its content. The song itself has endured numerous renditions, including a bagpipe version that was an international hit single.

Grace has almost become a cliché, a word we use to describe a table blessing ("saying grace") or use as a personal name. Beneath and beyond all of this, however, lies one of the most fundamental of all gospel truths—God lavishes undeserved favor, unearned benefits, and blessing on fallen human beings. Newton's hymn reflects the wonder of receiving such benefits not because of who he had been but in spite of who he had been. Like Paul, who has the most to say about grace in the New Testament, Newton had to experience grace before he was able to proclaim it.

A corollary to the grace side of this hymn needs to be recognized. When we are graced by God, we realize that we have been lost, unwittingly enmeshed in the clutches of sin and evil. Hindsight is a wonderful thing, but it is often painful to see how we have been in the past. We get the feeling that Newton winces as he reflects back on his connection with the slave trade and on the storms that wracked not only his boat but also his life. Sometimes we must come to the end of ourselves before we can come to the beginning of our relationship with God. It is only when we reach the end of our resources, pride, and strength that we realize we are not God. The sad fact is that some of us have to learn this lesson repeatedly. It is intriguing that Newton says he feared the God of grace, but grace also relieved his fears. Perhaps this is because Newton knew that even if God is gracious, sin must be rooted out and dealt with. Just as a surgeon who cares about us and wishes us long life must cut cancer out of our bodies, so it is with a gracious God. Those frightened of conversion or radical life transformation fear grace. But grace also relieves those fears.

Newton would have us always remember that God is gracious, not because of our inherent worth, but because grace is God's very nature. This is why in the last stanza Newton reminds us that God has promised good to us. God's totally reliable word secures our hopes. Though we may be faithless, God will be faithful as long as life endures. This is indeed amazing grace.

Questions for Reflection

What has this hymn meant to you in the past? Do you have any specific memories associated with its singing?

Which verse most resonates with your own personal experience? Why?

How have you been "blind" in your spiritual walk, and how has God brought you new insight?

What "dangers, toils, and snares" has God brought you through?

How have you experienced God's grace in your life?

Take time to look at your hopes and dreams for the future, and envision God's grace leading you and protecting you through every step.

NINE

Phillis Wheatley
(1753–84)

Transported from Africa to Boston as a seven-year-old slave, Phillis Wheatley was bought by Susanna Wheatley, a well-to-do, pious lady who saw that Phillis was taught English, Latin, and the Bible and who encouraged her writing. When a collection of Phillis's poems failed to interest a publisher in Boston, Mrs. Wheatley arranged for her to visit the Countess of Huntingdon in England. The countess's influence ensured that *Poems on Various Subjects, Religious and Moral,* with an engraved likeness of Phillis Wheatley as frontispiece, was published in London in 1773. This book is considered to be the first published by an African-American. On her return to Boston, however, Phillis had no success in getting subsequent volumes published.

On the Death of the Rev. Mr. George Whitefield. 1770

Hail, happy saint, on thine immortal throne,
Possest of glory, life, and bliss unknown;

We hear no more the music of thy tongue,
Thy wonted auditories cease to throng.
Thy sermons in unequall'd accents flow'd,   5
And ev'ry bosom with devotion glow'd;
Thou didst in strains of eloquence refin'd
Inflame the heart, and captivate the mind.
Unhappy we the setting sun deplore,
So glorious once, but ah! it shines no more.   10

Behold the prophet in his tow'ring flight!
He leaves the earth for heav'n's unmeasur'd height,

And worlds unknown receive him from our sight.
There *Whitefield* wings with rapid course his way,
And sails to *Zion* through vast seas of day.   15
Thy pray'rs, great saint, and thine incessant cries
Have pierc'd the bosom of thy native skies.
Thou moon hast seen, and all the stars of light,
How he has wrestled with his God by night.
He pray'd that grace in ev'ry heart might dwell,   20
He long'd to see *America* excel;
He charg'd its youth that ev'ry grace divine
Should with full lustre in their conduct shine;
That Saviour, which his soul did first receive,
The greatest gift that ev'n a God can give,   25
He freely offer'd to the num'rous throng,
That on his lips with list'ning pleasure hung.

    "Take him, ye wretched, for your only good,
"Take him ye starving sinners, for your food;
"Ye thirsty, come to this life-giving stream,   30
"Ye preachers, take him for your joyful theme;
"Take him my dear *Americans*, he said,
"Be your complaints on his kind bosom laid:
"Take him, ye *Africans*, he longs for you,
"*Impartial Saviour* is his title due: 35
"Wash'd in the fountain of redeeming blood,
"You shall be sons, and kings, and priests to God."

    Great *Countess*, we *Americans* revere
Thy name, and mingle in thy grief sincere;
New England deeply feels, the *Orphans* mourn,   40
Their more than father will no more return.

    But, though arrested by the hand of death,
Whitefield no more exerts his lab'ring breath,
Yet let us view him in th' eternal skies,
Let ev'ry heart to this bright vision rise;   45
While the tomb safe retains its sacred trust,
Till life divine re-animates his dust.

The Poetry

This poem by the "Sable Muse" was published in New England
in 1771 and in London in 1773. With the exception of one rhym-

ing triplet at lines 11–13, the poem is in the strict form of the heroic couplet that was so fashionable in the eighteenth century. Wheatley carefully maintains the ten-syllable iambic line by contracting words that could be pronounced with an extra syllable, as the four examples in lines 25–28 show. In one passage, she has Whitefield urging many kinds of people to accept Christ:

> "Take him my dear *Americans*, he said,
> "Be your complaints on his kind bosom laid:
> "Take him, ye *Africans*, he longs for you,
> "*Impartial Saviour* is his title due:
> "Wash'd in the fountain of redeeming blood,
> "You shall be sons, and kings, and priests to God." (lines 32–37)

The first of these couplets hints at colonial dissatisfaction with British rule, while the latter two express a yearning for emancipation from slavery. Wheatley visited England in 1773, partly to arrange for publication of a collection of her poems under the patronage of the Countess of Huntingdon (referred to in line 38). Slavery had been abolished in England, so Wheatley became legally free. She was then freed in America when she returned in 1774.

The Piety

This poem is in the form of an elegy or encomium for a dearly departed Christian friend and mentor. It reminds us that we stand on the shoulders of those who have gone before us. In fact, for those of us who are Christians, none of us would be what we are if someone had not shared the faith with us.

Certainly, one of the great pulpiteers of the eighteenth century was the man mourned in this poem—George Whitefield. Even the skeptical Benjamin Franklin reportedly said he would gladly trundle along in his bedclothes and listen to the Rev. Whitefield offer an ode to a flea, if needs be, so great an orator was he. Franklin also said that Whitefield could be heard for over a mile in downtown Philadelphia so great was his preaching voice. It is partly because of his abilities and their effects that Wheatley waxes eloquent about him.

Yet there is a great truth to be learned by looking a little further into the religious history of the matter. John Wesley was not

the eloquent orator that Whitefield was, but his preaching converted many, and unlike Whitefield, he had a great gift of organization. Near the end of his life, Whitefield even lamented how
the societies he had formed in imitation of Wesley's method had
become "a rope of sand" because they were not properly joined
together. Today, few Methodist churches testify to the legacy of
Whitefield, but many testify to the legacy of Wesley. Thus, this
poem reminds us that the battle is often won in the long run by
organization rather than eloquence. New wine, however effer-
vescent, without wineskins to contain and preserve it, has an effect only for a short while.

Another remarkable characteristic of this poem is its emphasis on the inclusiveness of God's grace in Christ for all people of
every race. We are told that Christ longs for Africans as much as
Americans. This is perhaps not a surprise considering that Wheatley
was an African-American. However, she was emphasizing this at
a time when the slave trade in America was increasing and many
were arguing that Africans were not fully human and could be
treated as property.

In the end, Whitefield is portrayed as a model for Christians to follow. Inasmuch as we become what we admire,
Wheatley presents for us a tableau of a faithful servant of
Christ whose zeal and efforts deserve to be emulated. In line
11 she compares him to Elijah the prophet ascending into
heaven, and at the end of the poem she reassures us that we
will see him again at the last resurrection. Thus, Whitefield
stands behind us as an example and before us as a witness
who will hold us accountable on the last day. Wheatley tran-
sitions from elegy to encomium at this point, reminding readers that we always stand in the presence of the communion of
the saints.

Questions for Reflection

It has been said "You become what you admire." Whom do you most
admire in this world? Why do you admire him or her? Reflect on
the admirable traits of this person, and then ask yourself, *In what
way do I emulate this example?*

It has also been said wine without wineskins is like revival without
organized discipleship thereafter. Why is order and organization

necessary for the Christian life? In what way does it complement Christian experience (e.g., of revival)?

What would happen if a person focused only on the high experiences of the Christian life and not on the discipline of obedience in day-to-day life? What would happen if a person focused only on duty and was not open to new life in the Spirit?

TEN

William Blake
(1757–1827)

Apprenticed to an engraver at age fourteen, William Blake also studied briefly at the Royal Academy of Art. After struggling to maintain a living as an artist, in 1800 he moved from London to Felpham on the coast of Sussex. There he worked under the patronage of William Hayley, but disagreements brought the arrangement to an end in 1803. Industrious and prolific as both poet and artist, Blake achieved little financial success, though in the last decade of his life he attracted some of the admiration that was to develop enormously in the twentieth century.

Jerusalem

And did those feet in ancient time
Walk upon England's mountains green?
And was the holy Lamb of God
On England's pleasant pastures seen?

And did the Countenance Divine   5
Shine forth upon our clouded hills?
And was Jerusalem builded here
Among these dark Satanic Mills?

Bring me my Bow of burning gold!
Bring me my Arrows of desire!   10
Bring me my Spear! O clouds, unfold!
Bring me my Chariot of fire!

I will not cease from Mental Fight,
Nor shall my Sword sleep in my hand,
Till we have built Jerusalem   15
In England's green and pleasant land.

The Poetry

This poem first appeared in the preface to Blake's prophetic poem *Milton* (1804). It subsequently acquired the title "Jerusalem" and is sung with much enthusiasm on various public occasions in England. The four questions in the first two quatrains implicitly reiterate the belief that Jesus visited England with Joseph of Arimathea. Since then, however, the grinding utilitarianism of the Industrial Revolution produced "dark Satanic Mills." This sterility can only be overcome by waging a vigorous spiritual warfare, expressed by the strikingly energetic and visionary imagery of the third and fourth quatrains. The destruction is not material; it is a "mental fight" requiring transformation within the individual, so that a New Jerusalem may be built in the poet's native land.

The Piety

According to John 4, Jesus said that wherever one worships God in spirit and in truth is a holy place. It is not a matter of making pilgrimage up to either Jerusalem or Mt. Gerizim. Thus, there is a limited sense in which Blake is right to endorse the myth that Joseph of Arimathea made England the New Jerusalem by bringing the holiest of vessels—the cup from the Last Supper—to that locale. Any and every land can be a holy land if there is true worship of the holy God there. Yet, this is not quite what Blake is suggesting. In fact, he implies that England (as opposed to France, for instance) has some sort of holy land status that is worth a holy "mental fight" to preserve. This romantic reaction to the rise of the Industrial Revolution is typical of that time. Industry is spoiling the Edenic nature of England. It amounts to a defiling of the holy. Nature is suffused with the divine and therefore should not be handled in a purely utilitarian manner.

But there is a fundamental confusion between the creation and the creator in such thinking. The natural world, while a good gift of God to his creatures, is not God nor is it always a vehicle of God's presence. It can, for instance, also be a vehicle of a different and more malevolent presence—evil. But precisely because nature is a gift from God, we must be good stewards of it, not abusing our earthly home. Consequently, there must be a mental sorting of what amounts to a use of nature that glorifies God and edifies humankind and what amounts to an abuse of nature. The proper use of nature is indeed a form of worshipping God in spirit and in truth—offering back to God what he has first given us.

Can we then hope to build the New Jerusalem by such salutary ecological efforts? According to Revelation 21, the answer must be no. The New Jerusalem, like the new heaven and the new earth (indeed, like the first creation), will be a gift from God. In the meantime, all ground can be hallowed ground if God is worshipped there, and all ground should be handled not as if it were divine but as a divine gift to us from God.

Questions for Reflection

> Have you ever felt like you were worshipping on holy ground? Where did this take place? What were the circumstances?
>
> What would it take to make the city in which you live more like a holy land? What can you do to bring God's holiness to your community?
>
> Look at the gift of nature God has given you in your neighborhood. Take time to thank God for these individual presents. What can you do to help preserve them?
>
> What "mental fight" do you face as you try to realize God's presence in your life?

ELEVEN

Sir Robert Grant
(1779–1838)

Robert Grant was born in India, graduated from Cambridge, and became a lawyer and a member of Parliament. He championed the movement to repeal the civil disabilities imposed on Jews. He was knighted and in 1834 was appointed governor of Bombay. He died in India four years later. His sacred poems were collected and published posthumously by his brother.

Glory and Goodness of God

O Worship the King all glorious above!
O gratefully sing his power and his love!
Our Shield and Defender—the Ancient of days,
Pavilion'd in splendor, and girded with praise.
O tell of his might, O sing of his grace!   5
Whose robe is the light—whose canopy space,
His chariots of wrath the deep thunder-clouds form,
And dark is his path on the wings of the storm.

The earth with its store of wonders untold,
Almighty! thy power hath founded of old;   10
Hath stablish'd it fast by a changeless decree,
And round it hath cast like a mantle the sea.
Thy bountiful care what tongue can recite?
It breathes in the air—it shines in the light;
In streams from the hills it descends to the plain   15
And sweetly distils in the dew and the rain.

> Frail children of dust, and feeble as frail,
> In thee do we trust, nor find thee to fail;
> Thy mercies how tender, how firm to the end,
> Our Maker, Defender, Redeemer, and Friend!   20
> O measureless Might—ineffable Love!
> While angels delight to hymn thee above,
> Thy humbler creation, though feeble their lays,
> With true adoration shall lisp to thy praise.

The Poetry

Published in 1835, this poem combines biblical language and imagery with the language and imagery of early-nineteenth-century Romanticism. The ornate language of "the Ancient of days / Pavilion'd in splendor, and girded with praise" (lines 3–4) and the traditional images in lines 10–12 and 22 have biblical echoes. The archaic use of "hath" in lines 10–12 reinforces the traditional effect.

By contrast, the language in the cosmic imagery of lines 6–8 and 14–16 is contemporary with the author. The five verbs *breathes, shines, streams, descends,* and *distills* in lines 14–16 are well chosen to represent the creator's bounty to his "frail children." Though their "feeble" expression of praise is a mere lisp, their relationship to God is not abject but benign (lines 20–21). The poem's elevated tone is aided by the weightiness of the lines, almost all of which have a major pause in the middle. Within each couplet, both lines have either ten or eleven syllables, further enhancing the theme of order and harmony.

The Piety

Whether it was the author's intent or not, the overall effect of this poem is to convey the majesty and awesome character of God. To that end there is an allusion to Ezekiel's throne-chariot vision (Ezek. 1) in which Ezekiel saw a thunderstorm coming and the very presence of God on his throne emerging from the storm, "pavilion'd in splendor." Part of this vision entailed the throne of God being held up by creatures which represented the whole of creation, in a sense lifting up God and offering him due homage and praise. The language of this hymn is appropriately exalted considering the subject matter it addresses.

The throne-chariot vision of Ezekiel also conveys the concepts of the omnipotence, omnipresence, and omniscience of God. Just when Ezekiel felt abandoned by God, God gave him a vision of the divine presence that showed he could be everywhere at once, was all-seeing, and was in control of his creation. These themes are alluded to in both stanzas one and two of Grant's hymn.

There is also a strong emphasis on God's paternal care for his children in the last two stanzas, again echoing the prophet's encounter with God in Ezekiel 1. Bear in mind that Ezekiel is often called "son of man," and he is portrayed as the frail and vulnerable representative human being. His words are feeble, inadequate to sufficiently praise the God who cared enough to come to him in his captivity. While it is true that the language of this hymn draws on reverie of the Romantic period with its deliberate archaizing and longing for halcyon days of old, it seems probable the writer is trying to echo a much earlier period of history as well—the age of the Hebrew prophets and their piety. In this hymn, as in the vision of Ezekiel, there is a salutary reminder that the creator-creature distinction needs to be preserved and is the very basis of worship, for worship is something offered to a being so much more exalted than we are that it is appropriate to bow down before such a one.

Questions for Reflection

Read Ezekiel 1, and reread the first stanza of the poem. Imagine you had witnessed this vision of God. What would you be feeling? How would you react? Which description is closest to how you see God—maker, defender, redeemer, or friend? Which is furthest? Why?

What evidence of God's "bountiful care" do you witness around you?

As one of God's "frail children of dust," what aspect of your life makes you feel most frail? Take a few minutes to offer this frailty up to God, asking him to help you trust his firm, tender mercies to the end.

TWELVE

John Henry Newman
(1801–90)

Ordained in the Church of England, John Henry Newman was
one of the leaders of the Oxford Movement in the 1830s, which
argued for the doctrine of apostolic succession and the integrity
of the Book of Common Prayer. By 1845, however, he had joined
the Church of Rome, was ordained in it in 1846, and was made
a cardinal in 1879. "Lead, Kindly Light" was composed during a
voyage from Palermo to Marseilles in 1833.

Lead, Kindly Light

Lead, kindly light, amid the encircling gloom,
 Lead thou me on;
The night is dark, and I am far from home;
 Lead thou me on.
Keep thou my feet; I do not ask to see   5
The distant scene: one step enough for me.

I was not ever thus, nor prayed that thou
 Shouldst lead me on;
I loved to choose and see my path; but now
 Lead thou me on.   10
I loved the garish day, and, spite of fears,
Pride ruled my will: remember not past years.

So long thy power hath blest me, sure it still
 Will lead me on
O'er moor and fen, o'er crag and torrent, till   15
 The night is gone,

And with the morn those angel faces smile
Which I have loved long since, and lost awhile.

The Poetry

This hymn is unusual in that the short second and fourth lines, which reiterate the dominant idea, serve as a refrain in the middle of each six-line stanza. Most of the longer lines also divide into two short phrases suitable for setting to music. The speaker expresses a penitent attitude for his egotistical assertiveness in the past and his present disenchantment with the world. It is depicted in terms of nature—"moor and fen," "crag and torrent"—each phrase preceded with the poetic contraction "o'er." More hopefully, the concluding couplet anticipates a reunion with dead loved ones in the next life.

The Piety

This interesting hymn takes as its starting point the idea that we live in a dark and dangerous world, but a bright light can lead us home. Notice how Newman only asks for enough light to illumine the path in front of him. It may be true that sometimes God does not give us what we ask because it has to do with the more distant future and more remote needs than those that need to be addressed today.

Notice, too, that Newman freely admits he has at times failed to recognize his need to be led, his need for the light. At some point in our lives, most of us have attempted to be the captains of our own fates, choosing our own paths. God will often allow us to reap the consequences of our actions so we will see and learn from our mistakes. Newman, however, asks that God not judge him or at least not react on the basis of his past behavior. In other words, Newman recognizes that God's mercies are new each morning and God is ready to forgive and start afresh with us. To ask for light for the day and to trust God for the future is indeed a good way for pilgrims to live if they wish to eventually find their way home.

Questions for Reflection

Are you closer to God today than you were five years ago? Why or why not?

When has pride caused you to stray from God?

Meditate for a few minutes on the idea that God's mercies are new every morning. How does that make you feel? Take time to praise God for his mercy.

List all of your prayer concerns. Now look and see which are prayers for today and which involve more long-term requests. Reword the latter to address the portion of problems that can be dealt with today.

THIRTEEN

Christina Rossetti
(1830–94)

Christina Rossetti was the younger sister of Dante Gabriel and William Michael Rossetti, children of an Italian patriot in exile in England. They grew up in a home vibrant with political and cultural interests and became prominent in the Pre-Raphaelite group of artists. A devout Anglican, Christina broke off her engagement to a Pre-Raphaelite painter who had rejoined the Roman Catholic Church, and she never married. Devoted to her family and charitable work, she published numerous works, many designed for children.

Easter Monday

Out in the rain a world is growing green,
  On half the trees quick buds are seen
    Where glued-up buds have been.
Out in the rain God's Acre stretches green,
  Its harvest quick tho' still unseen: 5
    For there the Life hath been.

If Christ hath died His brethren well may die,
  Sing in the gate of death, lay by
    This life without a sigh:
For Christ hath died and good it is to die;   10
  To sleep when so He lays us by,
    Then wake without a sigh.

Yea, Christ hath died, yea, Christ is risen again:
  Wherefore both life and death grow plain
    To us who wax and wane;   15

97

> For Christ Who rose shall die no more again:
> Amen: till He makes all things plain
> Let us wax on and wane.

The Poetry

In this poem, Christina Rossetti employs several verbal devices to reinforce the theme of resurrection. Each six-line stanza opens with a triple rhyme and then repeats the three end-words as the triple rhyme in the second half of the stanza. Similarly, the first four words in the first and fourth line of each stanza are nearly identical, as are the last three or four words of the third and sixth lines. This intricate recurring or reviving is appropriate to the theme of resurrection. Another feature is the opposition between such words as *death, die, died,* and *sleep,* and *life, risen, rose, wake,* and *quick* (originally meaning alive, as in "the quick and the dead"). "God's Acre" in line 4 is the graveyard from which the "unseen" dead will become a "harvest quick" at the resurrection. In the meantime, our mortal life cycles will continue as we "wax and wane."

The Piety

Rossetti's poem suggests that things are not always as they seem. More to the point, since Christ's resurrection, we must never take for granted that anything is quite as it seems. If even death can be cheated, then while life may be invisible or hidden for a time, this does not mean it has ceased to exist. Christ, the firstfruits of the resurrection, is not merely the harbinger of our resurrection. He is the guarantor that a similar destiny awaits the believer.

Thus, death is transfigured into something more like a rest or a sleep from which the believer awakes alive and refreshed. This being so, the believer may in trust and hope watch the natural life wane without undue worry or fear. God's yes to life is louder than death's no, and we will one day "wake without a sigh." Yet, these things will not be made plain until the resurrection.

Questions for Reflection

Observe some things that are not as they seem.
Think of a time when God's promises seemed hidden or far away.

How has God revealed his promises since then? How do you expect God to fulfill these promises in the future?

What fears of death do you have?

Reflect on God's promises of resurrection (e.g., 1 Thess. 4:13–17), and ask God to make these the primary images of death/life for you.

FOURTEEN

Thomas Hardy
(1840–1928)

During Thomas Hardy's long life, religious faith was continually eroding under the impact of geological discoveries and evolutionary theory. He abandoned an early inclination to take holy orders and became an architect. Ironically, his work mainly consisted of restoring churches. Gradually, however, the growing success of his novels, especially *Far From the Madding Crowd* (1874), enabled him to earn his living by writing. After criticism for his alleged immorality in *Tess of the D'Urbervilles* (1891) and *Jude the Obscure* (1895), Hardy wrote no more novels but devoted himself to poetry.

The Oxen

Christmas Eve, and twelve of the clock.
    "Now they are all on their knees,"
An elder said as we sat in a flock
    By the embers in hearthside ease.

We pictured the meek mild creatures where   5
    They dwelt in their strawy pen,
Nor did it occur to one of us there
    To doubt they were kneeling then.

So fair a fancy few would weave
    In these years! Yet, I feel,   10
If someone said on Christmas Eve,
    "Come; see the oxen kneel,

"In the lonely barton by yonder coomb
    Our childhood used to know,"
I should go with him in the gloom,   15
    Hoping it might be so.

The Poetry

This poem evokes a mood of yearning for the faith of a bygone era. The setting of an "elder" speaking to a group creates an atmosphere typical of a religious gathering. This context is enhanced in the second quatrain by the image of animals kneeling beside a manger, especially with the unusual adjective "strawy" and the archaic diction of line 13. The alliteration at the start of the third quatrain draws attention to the reflective exclamation there. The effect of the long vowels in the fourth quatrain, especially in the monosyllables, is heightened by the change of meter with "hoping" in the last line. The hope of rediscovering the childhood vision of Christ's nativity is poignantly articulated.

The Piety

This poem is perfect for an age of agnosticism, plagued by doubt yet longing for a substantial faith. The poem conveys an air of wistfulness, even reverie, as if the Christmas story were a childhood fairy tale the adult poet now wishes he could still believe. Part of the problem, of course, is that a good deal of what passes for the Christmas story is the stuff of myth and legend which the Gospels do not record or even suggest. Like a painting that has been given a protective coating of lacquer only to have the lacquer age and fade and discolor the original painting, so it is with the legendary accretions to the Gospel stories. For example, in Hardy's poem the animals kneel at the manger of the Christ child, something Christmas carols may suggest (e.g., "Good Christian Men Rejoice"), but the Bible does not.

In a skeptical age, of course, it is all too easy to throw the baby out with the bath water. Perhaps we would be well served to return *ad fontes* and rethink the matter, for true faith does not require belief in legendary accretions to a historical account, only trust in the original story itself. The great tragedy is that some have mistaken the lacquer for the very substance of the painting.

Because the latter seemed obviously off-color, they feel relieved of the responsibility of dealing with the original masterpiece. Nevertheless, beneath the tarnished Christmas story that is served up each year with too much sentiment and too little substance, there lies a challenging reality.

Let us deal first with the issue of truths learned in childhood (the last quatrain). The Christian faith is said to be simple enough for a child to grasp but profound enough for an adult to grapple with. There is, however, a difference between a childlike faith and a childish faith, a simple faith and a simpleton's faith, which believes in spite of the evidence. Hardy longs to return to a faith in what "our childhood used to know," but in the gloom of the modern age, he is not sure whether it is possible to get there from where he is as an adult. In other words, he fears that the sacrifice required of his intellect may be too great. Ironically, the Christmas story does not require him to believe in animals kneeling reverently; it requires him to believe that an all-powerful God chose to visit us in the person of his Son. We may talk about the scandal of the gospel and the leap of faith, but neither faith nor doubt should be based on elements that are not part of the original story. We need to know the story before we accept or reject it. Furthermore, we need to closely examine the pith of the story.

Second, let us consider the original story in Luke 2:4–7. Joseph and Mary must return to Bethlehem, Joseph's ancestral home, to be registered for tax purposes. Bethlehem was a small town that might not have had a wayside inn. Whether it did or not, the likely place a poor couple would stay when making such a visit, especially with a pregnant woman involved, was with Joseph's relatives. The Greek word in question in Luke 2:7, *kataluma*, while it can mean "inn," has a more common meaning of "guest room." This is precisely what it means elsewhere in Luke and Acts, including the story of the Last Supper. Furthermore, Luke uses a different word for "inn" in the parable of the Good Samaritan.

What happens to our story if we make a simple and likely variation in the translation of *kataluma*? First, no image is conveyed of the holy family being told there is no room in a wayside inn.

What they learn is that they have arrived at their relatives too late to be accommodated in the guest room. But this is not the end of the matter. Far too many Christmas sermons have been based on the assumption that the family then ended up in a barn. This too is doubtful. In ancient Israel, peasant families, having only a few precious farm animals, regularly brought those animals into the back of their homes for safekeeping, especially at night and in winter. Historically, it is far more plausible that Joseph's relatives made room for the holy family in the back or lower part of their home where the animals were. In short, the whole idea of the holy family being cast out by the world is probably not part of the original story.

Finally, notice that Luke 2:7 makes no mention of animals being present, unlike the story beginning in Luke 2:8, which is set out in the fields where there are shepherds and sheep. It is entirely possible that Mary's placing Jesus in the manger is an act that bespeaks the absence of animals in the home at this time. Hardy's animals were likely not even present at the birth, never mind their doing obeisance!

When we allow the Christmas story and its legendary accretions to blend together in our minds, we miss the original thrust of the story, and we mislead those who would like to believe in it. John Donne understood the heart of the story: "Twas much that man was made like God before; / But that God should be made like man—much more." The Christmas story does not call us back to a faith in the fractured fairy tales of childhood. It calls us forward to deal with the miracle of the incarnation. If there is to be mental wrestling in this age of doubt, let it be with the real substance of the real story.

Questions for Reflection

Compare your own family tradition for "Christmas Eve, and twelve of the clock" with that of the poet.

What traditional image of the Christmas story is foremost in your mind? Why? Compare this image with those found in Luke 2:1–20.

Think about a truth of the Christian faith that was simple enough for you to grasp as a child (or when you first became a Christian) but which you now find profound enough to grapple with. What challenges you most about this concept? How is it also a simple truth?

Is there any aspect of the Christmas story that you find particularly difficult to believe? Write down your doubts and fears, and then ask God to help you understand this area better.

FIFTEEN

Gerard Manley Hopkins
(1844–89)

As a student at Highgate School in London, Gerard Manley Hopkins won a prize for his poem "The Escorial." He studied classics at Balliol College, Oxford, and earned first-class honors in 1867. At Oxford, his interest in Catholicism was greatly influenced by John Henry Newman. Despite strong opposition by his parents, Hopkins became a Roman Catholic and was ordained as a Jesuit priest in 1877. He had burned his early poems because they were too worldly, but he was encouraged by his superior to write a poem about the wreck of the *Deutschland* in which five nuns drowned. Hopkins served as a priest and teacher in several locations and in 1884 was appointed professor of classics at University College, Dublin. Overwhelmed by administrative and academic work, he expressed his spiritual torment in the "Terrible Sonnets." He died of typhoid at the age of forty-four. Very few of his poems were published during his lifetime. However, when his friend Robert Bridges brought out a collection of Hopkins's poems in 1918, he soon acquired a fame that continues.

Heaven-Haven
A nun takes the veil

I have desired to go
Where springs not fail,
To fields where flies no sharp and sided hail
And a few lilies blow.

And I have asked to be   5
Where no storms come,
Where the green swell is in the havens dumb,
And out of the swing of the sea.

The Poetry

The compactness of this early poem by Hopkins suggests the deliberateness of the nun's choice of vocation. She wishes to leave behind the storms and uncertainties of the natural world in favor of the anticipated certitude of devoting herself to God. Yet the main clauses, "I have desired to go" and "I have asked to be," express only a wish, not a confident or dogmatic assertion of faith.

The Piety

The psalmist says, "Be still and know that I am God." In this spinning world, there is no point more still than a sanctuary, particularly one within a cloister, monastery, or convent. One of the most interesting things about Hopkins's simple verse is that the speaker talks not only of what she desires to leave behind but also of what she wishes to find when she gets there—an Eden of perpetual spring, where no storms can be found, where nothing dark and dangerous can touch her, and where beauty and purity (symbolized by the lily) always greet her.

The convent then is a picture of a paradise, but like the Garden of Eden, it is surrounded by a wild world. The haven is like heaven with no present evil, but it is unlike heaven with danger lurking just beyond its walls. It is interesting that in the Book of Revelation, even as the clean, pure New Jerusalem appears on earth, the unclean and those who practice abominations still lurk just outside its walls (21:27). Good and evil always seem to be in close proximity, whether in paradise lost or paradise regained. These images and ideas do not seek to solve the questions of good and evil. Rather, they are meant to reassure the faithful of protection from evil both now and in the end.

Throughout the Old Testament era, there is a concept of sanctuary. An individual being pursued could obtain at least temporary respite from the pursuer by entering the tent of meeting and grasping the horns of the altar. At that point, the individual had sanctuary. This custom continued into the Middle Ages when the doorknocker on the cathedral served in place of the horns of the altar. There is, of course, a paradox in this idea. Though we may escape the enemy without, we cannot escape the enemy within. Indeed, when we seek sanctuary, we run straight into the earthly locus of the judge of all humankind. The nun in the poem looks for relief and respite, for sanctuary, but she says nothing about being prepared to worship in that sanctuary. Perhaps she is like many of us. Weary of the world's evil, we seek sanctuary, but we are not quite ready to come into the presence of everlasting goodness and holiness. Yet she is looking for beauty and purity in the created order, and we must see her as being on pilgrimage toward the ultimate end, even though she believes she is entering a heaven-haven.

Questions for Reflection

Where do you go to find sanctuary, silence, peace, and quiet?

When you get to that special place, what do you do with your time there? Do you read your Bible, pray, reflect?

It has been said that no matter how far you run, you cannot outrun your own skin. Do you agree with this or not?

What do you take the verse "Be still and know that I am God" to mean? Take time to write about how you "practice the presence of God." How could you improve your times in your special haven or sanctuary?

The Windhover:
To Christ Our Lord

I caught this morning morning's minion,
　　kingdom of daylight's dauphin, dapple-dawn-drawn Falcon,
　　　in his riding
Of the rolling level underneath him steady air, and striding
High there, how he rung upon the rein of a wimpling wing
In his ecstasy! then off, off forth on swing,　　　　　　　5
　　As a skate's heel sweeps smooth on a bow-bend: the hurl
　　　and gliding
　　Rebuffed the big wind. My heart in hiding
Stirred for a bird,—the achieve of, the mastery of the thing!

Brute beauty and valour and act, oh, air, pride, plume here
    Buckle! And fire that breaks from thee then, a billion   10
    Times told lovelier, more dangerous, O my chevalier!

    No wonder of it: shéer plód makes plough down sillion
Shine, and blue-beak embers, ah my dear,
    Fall, gall themselves, and gash gold-vermilion.

The Poetry

In a letter to Robert Bridges, who became his posthumous editor, Hopkins called this poem "the best thing I ever wrote." As usual in his sonnets, he follows the Italian form of eight and six lines. The octave recreates the way the windhover, a small falcon also known as a kestrel, hovers in the air while seeking prey.

In the title of the poem, "Windhover" is followed by a colon, thus raising the question of whether "To Christ Our Lord" is a dedication or is part of the poem. If the latter, there is particular emphasis on Christ's beauty and power and how they permeate creation, in this instance in the bird. This interconnectedness, so central to Hopkins's view of the world, is reflected throughout the poem: in the corresponding qualities of falcon, chevalier, horse, and plow, and in the multiple meanings of several key words and images.

The opening two words, "I caught," can suggest both "caught sight of" and "captured the essence of" the bird. The imagery in the first four lines is drawn from chivalry. The speaker sees the falcon as its darling ("minion"), as the princely heir to the French throne ("dauphin"), and in line 11 as a "chevalier." In the knightly sport of falconry, "rung up on the rein" meant that the falcon was allowed to ascend from the human wrist in spirals. The phrase can also apply to training a horse by using a long rein that makes it move in circles. "Wimpling" means rippling, an apt term for the falcon's hovering wings. The swerving, circular motion is continued in the image of the skater sweeping round in a bow pattern (line 6).

The connectedness of the falcon and the knight is sustained through the six nouns in line 9, linked by the verb "Buckle!" It has several meanings that can apply in this context: buckle on armor; join; apply vigorously (as in "buckle down to a task");

grapple; and conversely, bend, crumple, or submit. Either way, the divine energy ("fire") and loveliness of the poet's chevalier, Christ, are infinitely ("a billion times") more powerful than those of any creature. According to Paul Mariari, these three lines allude both to the way the falcon's wings assume a V-shape as it swoops down on its prey and to Christ's shape on the cross.[1] The final three lines show how Christ's "beauty and valour and act" may be replicated at humble human levels. As the plodding plowman pushes the plow, it shines as it is driven down the narrow strip of land between two furrows ("sillion," a spelling of "selion" not given in the *Oxford English Dictionary*); and embers, even as they disintegrate, reveal their fiery ("gold-vermilion") colors.

The Piety

"Windhover" is certainly one of the most memorable of Hopkins's poems, not least because of its celebration of beauty and freedom. It is worth reflecting for a moment on how the kestrel itself is an image of Christ. Bird images of the divine are not unknown in the Bible (e.g., Christ as a mother bird in Matt. 23:37–38). Yet the kestrel is a bird of prey—dangerous though beautiful. Even so, we can compare the image of God as an eagle in Ezekiel 17:1–15. There the image suggests not merely God's sovereignty and freedom but his power to judge his own people. The tone of judgment is absent from Hopkins's poem. Rather, the emphasis is on beauty, grace, style, power, and freedom. Hopkins is fascinated with the bird and its mobility much as the prophet was fascinated with the beauty and mobility of God in his apocalyptic vision (see Ezek. 1–2).

There is more here than meets the eye. The bird is exercising its skills against the wind, and yet it is able to master its environment and circumstances. This is indeed an appropriate image for Christ the Lord, who against the strong prevailing wind of evil was able to rise up beyond death and ascend into the heavens, much like the kestrel. The usual image of the risen Christ is the phoenix rising from the ashes. But since Hopkins's focus is on creation the-

---

1. *A Commentary on the Complete Poems of Gerard Manley Hopkins* (Ithaca, N.Y.: Cornell University Press, 1970), 12.

ology rather than victory beyond death, the image of a bird full of power and life best suits his purposes. Thus, this poem not only celebrates creation but the mastery of the creator over his creation. Hopkins is captivated by this act of sovereignty and control. Indeed, he is caught up in the moment and is led to a sort of doxology as suggested in the poem's subtitle.

Questions for Reflection

What other images in nature speak to you of the mastery of the creator over his creation?

Take time now to thank God for the magnificence of his creation.

What characteristics of the falcon seem to best parallel the characteristics of Christ?

What are some practical ways you can imitate Christ's "beauty and valour and act" as you interact with your family, friends, and co-workers this week?

Pied Beauty

Glory be to God for dappled things—
   For skies of couple-colour as a brinded cow;
     For rose-moles all in stipple upon trout that swim;
Fresh-firecoal chestnut-falls; finches' wings;
   Landscape plotted and pieced—fold, fallow, and plough;   5
     And áll trádes, their gear and tackle and trim.

All things counter, original, spare, strange;
   Whatever is fickle, freckled (who knows how?)
     With swift, slow; sweet, sour; adazzle, dim;
He fathers-forth whose beauty is past change: 10
   Praise him.

The Poetry

"Pied Beauty" is an example of the *curtal sonnet*. Instead of consisting of eight- and six-line sections, it has six and four lines rhyming *abcabc dbcd* followed by a very short line rhyming *c*. The lines have an irregular number of syllables in accord with what Hopkins called "sprung rhythm," a meter based on the stressed syllables in a line without regard to the number of un-stressed ones and therefore like the rhythm of ordinary speech.

Into this compact verse, Hopkins packs a catalogue of items in the world whose beauty and individuality attest to the infinite creativity of God. As usual, he seeks to bring out the inscape (see commentary on "God's Grandeur" for a definition) by employing vigorous language abounding with alliteration and assonance; oxymorons ("swift, slow; sweet, sour; adazzle, dim"); and unexpected accents ("áll trádes"). By its conciseness, the last line emphasizes Hopkins's devotion to the creator.

The Piety

This poem is a doxology and resonates with various praise psalms that focus on creation (e.g., Ps. 8). Like the psalmist, Hopkins is in awe of the variegated reality that is nature. Patterns in the clouds remind him of patterns on cows or moles on a trout. A burst of colorful sparks in a coal fire is coupled with brightly colored finches' wings. Thus far, the poet is simply reflecting on patterns beyond human contrivance or creation. Hopkins is not just indulging in free association but contemplating and glorying in the intricacy that suggests a divine hand on all of creation.

As in Psalm 8, Hopkins sees humankind as the crown of creation. In the last two lines of the first stanza, he reflects on the work of human hands that plots and pieces landscapes into certain patterns of planted or fallow ground. Farming is not the only task that draws us near to God; indeed, all trades and all the gear involved in them bring us closer to him. Underlying all of this is a theology of the goodness of work. Humans are, under God, mini-creators of beauty, and so God should be praised for creating beings capable of such activities.

In the second stanza, we are reminded of God's reply to Job (Job 38). Job is informed that just because he does not understand all the hows and whys of creation, it does not mean there is not a design and purpose to it all. Hopkins does not offer a protest as Job did, but he does wonder about things such as how freckles happen and why strange things were created in the first place. The scope of creation is shown by the antinomies of sweet and sour, swift and slow, brilliant and dull. Hopkins revels in the odd as well as the awesome. God sires all of this. Yet in the midst of and behind this kaleidoscope of creation, there stands an unchanging being whose beauty is beyond change. In short, all the fading beauty of creation is but a reflection of his unfolding beauty. The poem begins and ends with doxology, for God is the Alpha and Omega of all creation and all beauty.

Questions for Reflection

What in your mind is the most awesome sight in all of creation?

Christianity has a specific doctrine of creation that distinguishes the creator from what he has made. This means that creation has at most a reflected glory; it is not innately divine. How does this affect the way you look at nature?

Consider the intricacy of a spider's web. Ponder how the spider knows to weave it in such a pattern. Do you believe God has programmed nature in a particular way to reflect his beauty, intricacy, and orderliness?

Take time to read Job 38–42. Can you relate to Job's response?

God's Grandeur

The world is charged with the grandeur of God.
  It will flame out, like shining from shook foil;
  It gathers to a greatness, like the ooze of oil
Crushed. Why do men then now not reck his rod?
Generations have trod, have trod, have trod;   5
  And all is seared with trade; bleared, smeared with toil;
  And wears man's smudge and shares man's smell: the soil
Is bare now, nor can foot feel, being shod.

And for all this, nature is never spent;
  There lives the dearest freshness deep down things;   10
And though the last lights off the black West went
  Oh, morning, at the brown brink eastward, springs—
Because the Holy Ghost over the bent
  World broods with warm breast and with ah! bright wings.

The Poetry

This poem is at the same time orthodox and unconventional. In form it adheres to the pattern of the Italian sonnet, rhyming *abbaabba cdcdcd* and having ten syllables in every line. In diction and meter, however, it exhibits several unusual features that stem from Hopkins's unique poetic theory and practice.

The opening line immediately breaks the mold of iambic pentameter since it has only four stressed words: *world, charged, grandeur,* and *God.* The second line has four or five stresses, depending on whether the reader stresses *flame* and *out, shook* and *fail* as well as *shining.* The metaphor in these two lines illustrates Hopkins's belief that divine energy operates throughout creation. He once wrote, "I mean foil in its sense of leaf or tinsel. . . . Shaken goldfoil gives off broad glares like sheet lightning and also, and this is true of nothing else, owing to its zig-zag dints and creasings and network of small cornered facets, a sort of fork lightning too."[2] The verb "charged" reinforces the sense of electric power.

Hopkins considered that a thing had an individually distinctive set of qualities, for which he coined the term *inscape.* In order to express this individuality, he treated language unconventionally, especially by employing what he called "sprung rhythm." In this technique, meter is based on the stressed syllables in a line without regard to the number of unstressed syllables.

He also uses other devices to achieve vitality in language. In the first four lines, for example, alliteration occurs in phrases such as "grandeur of God," "flame . . . like shining from shook foil," "gathers to a greatness," and "reck his rod," and assonance occurs in the "ooze of oil." The remaining ten lines contain similar examples. The thrice-repeated "have trod" in line 5 and the words "seared," "bleared," "smeared" in line 6 effectively convey Hopkins's sense of the tedium in modern life, an idea echoed in "wears man's smudge and shares man's smell." The last four lines of the octave reinforce this effect by containing thirty-four monosyllables and closing with the dull thud of "shod."

The sestet immediately establishes a counterargument with the colloquial phrase, "And for all this." Alliteration and assonance continue to lend emphasis, this time to the endlessly restorative power of nature as presided over by the Holy Ghost. Hopkins dares to express his emotion by using the expletives "oh" and "ah," ending this sonnet with the upbeat "ah! bright wings."

2. *The Letters of Gerard Manley Hopkins to Robert Bridges,* ed. C. C. Abbott (London and New York: Oxford University Press, 1955), 169.

The Piety

This poem is a far more complex piece of work than "Pied Beauty," and it serves as a nice counterbalance to it. If "Pied Beauty" was an ode to the God of creation, Hopkins now goes a step further and reflects not just on creation but on creation affected by the fall. Work has become toil, and the beauty of the landscape has become smudged and smeared. Trade, which was seen as a good thing in the previous poem, is now portrayed as an agent of drudgery and a way of imposing our human fallenness, our very smell, on all of creation. The last line of the first stanza is especially telling. Hopkins reminds us of that aboriginal time when humans went unshod in the garden and were in full harmony and touch with nature. But now, one step removed, we cannot feel the fellowship with the soil and so are destined to trample it into submission. While the world is charged with grandeur, we have crushed it by our heedless stride. Yet the cry, "Why do men then now not reck his rod?" (that is, heed his authority), provides the answer to why this is all happening and the way back to appreciating and living in harmony with the good earth and its creator.

In the sestet, Hopkins returns to the theme of creation, emphasizing its resiliency in light of the fall. The good news is that there is an "and yet" that is not just based on the fact that nature has been encoded with vast hidden resources. God in the person of the Holy Spirit continues to renew creation day after day. If the fading of light and darkness are emblems of the fall, then sunrise is a symbol of re-creation. Obviously, the last two lines echo the beginning of the creation story as God's Spirit broods over the deep, ready to bring order out of chaos. Here the Holy Spirit, as at Jesus' baptism in Mark 1, is depicted as a dove with warm breast and bright wings, a mother bird warming the eggs beneath her, about to give birth to another new creature. In short, we have a tale of creation, fall, and redemption, the three great acts of the biblical drama, with the poet concluding with an emphasis on re-creation.

In this beautiful and challenging poem, we have an inkling of a proper ecologically minded theology that is concerned with the care and renewal of the earth. In addition, we get a glimpse of the almost ecstatic nature of Hopkins's piety, for he is clearly enraptured by the beauty of creation and by the creative Spirit, "caught up in wonder, love, and praise." The monastic life no doubt placed him closer to nature in its pristine state, and so some would say, closer to God.

Questions for Reflection

What most disturbs you about human wastefulness? Have you personally experienced the spoiling of the environment? What obligations do you think humans should have as stewards and conservers of the earth?

In what way do you see the Holy Spirit renewing creation on an ongoing basis?

Carefully read Romans 8:19–23. In what way does Paul suggest the creation and humankind are linked? In what way are the future of the earth and humanity intertwined according to Paul? Relate this Romans passage to some of Hopkins's reflections in this poem.

Thou Art Indeed Just, Lord, If I Contend

Justus quidem tu es, Domine, si disputem tecum: verumtamen justa loquar ad te: Quare via impiorum prosperatur? etc.

Thou art indeed just, Lord, if I contend
With thee; but, sir, so what I plead is just.
Why do sinners' ways prosper? and why must
Disappointment all I endeavor end?
Wert thou my enemy, O thou my friend, 5
How wouldst thou worse, I wonder, than thou dost
Defeat, thwart me? Oh, the sots and thralls of lust
Do in spare hours more thrive than I that spend,
Sir, life upon thy cause. See, banks and brakes
Now, leavèd how thick! lacèd they are again 10
With fretty chervil, look, and fresh wind shakes
Them; birds build—but not I build; no, but strain,
Time's eunuch, and not breed one work that wakes.
Mine, O thou lord of life, send my roots rain.

The Poetry

This is one of the "terrible" sonnets that Hopkins wrote near the end of his life, expressing uncertainty and anguish about his

religious calling. The title and the Latin epigraph are cited from
Jeremiah 12:1. The Latin is from the Vulgate and may be trans-
lated as follows: "Righteous art thou, O Lord, when I complain
to thee; yet let me talk with thee about thy judgments. Why does
the way of the wicked prosper? etc." The "etc." suggests that
Hopkins intended subsequent verses to be borne in mind, and
several of them have particular relevance to him and to the imagery of this sonnet.

Hopkins's conversion to Roman Catholicism strained his relationship with his Anglican family. "I have forsaken my house, I
have abandoned my heritage" (Jer. 12:7) is matched in the poem
by "I . . . spend / Sir, life upon thy cause" (line 9). Subsequently,
he became a Jesuit priest and gave up writing poetry because it
could be construed as a self-indulgent pleasure that would con-
flict with his priestly duties. This situation is perhaps reflected
in Jeremiah 12:10: "Many shepherds have destroyed my vineyard, they have trampled down my portion, they have made my
pleasant portion a desolate wilderness." Encouraged by his superior, Hopkins eventually did write poetry again, as this sonnet
from his later life attests.

The first three lines serve as a translation of the Latin epigraph. The epithet "Sir" for God suggests the respect required of
a litigant toward a judge and has a formality different from the
more personal tone Hopkins adopts in line 5: "Wert thou my enemy, O thou my friend." The first quatrain closes with the word
"end" echoing the word "endeavour."

The bitter complaint, "Oh, the sots and thralls [prisoners] of
lust / Do in spare hours more thrive than I" reiterates Hopkins's
explanation as to why he has delayed in answering a letter from
Robert Bridges: "Time and spirit were wanting: one is so fagged,
so harried and gallied [galled] up and down. And the drunkards
go on drinking, the filthy, as the scripture says, are filthy still:
human nature is so inveterate."

The spring imagery of lines 9–12 can be related to Jeremiah
12:2: "Thou plantest them, and they take root; they grow and
bring forth fruit; thou art near in their mouth but far from
their heart" (RSV). The unexpected lyrical uplift of spring
(from "See, banks and brakes / Now, leavèd how thick!" to
"birds build") contrasts with the final two and a half lines,

where the poet laments his sterility and prays to the "lord of life" to revitalize him.

The Piety

One kind of Christian piety suggests the Christian should be a Stoic, never complaining or saying a discouraging word about the slings and arrows of outrageous fortune in this life. Whatever may be said about the virtues of such a grin-and-bear-it attitude, it has no solid biblical foundation. Consider, for example, that the largest single category of psalms in the Bible is the lament or complaint. There are both individual and corporate laments (e.g., Pss. 22, 74, and 94). Compared to some of these psalms, the "terrible sonnets" seem tame.

First, note to whom Hopkins takes his complaint—the God he still can call friend. It is not an act of impiety to share our hearts with God, even when our hearts are full of pain and questions. Job's fault was not his complaining but rather his doubting of God's justice and fairness. Hopkins is not quite there, for he says he is "time's eunuch." In other words, he is going through an empty or sterile time, a dry period in his spiritual life. Yet this sonnet shows that when the ground is dry, it is time to put down deeper roots in our relationships to the fertile source of all being.

When bad things happen to God's people, it often creates a sense of distance or detachment between believers and the Lord. Hopkins is certainly experiencing that, for he calls God "Sir," which shows respect but also suggests being one step removed from the intimacy with God that permeates many of his earlier poems. Hopkins feels thwarted and unable to create as he had in the past.

Ironically, in this sonnet, Hopkins turns his pain into a creative expression of entreaty to God. In the final line, God is still called "lord of life," and Hopkins still believes it is possible for heaven-sent rain to fertilize his imagination and life once more. Like most of the laments in the Psalter, this sonnet turns from imprecation to entreaty. Hopkins does not know and fears what the future may hold, yet he knows who holds the future. So he addresses this sonnet to the one capable of providing remedy and redemption.

Questions for Reflection

Is your spiritual life currently in a dry period, or are you experiencing the "banks and brakes" of spring?

What is the biggest complaint you have brought or need to bring to God?

What signs of refreshing are present in your life now?

If you are experiencing dryness, take time now to pour out your lament to God. If you are experiencing a new spring, thank God for his replenishing Spirit.

Read Psalm 22. Meditate on how, in times of weariness, God can change your cry of despair into a cry of victory.

SIXTEEN

Francis Thompson
(1859–1907)

Francis Thompson was born into a Roman Catholic family and was educated in that faith at Upshaw College near Manchester, England. Because of his poor health and dreamy nature, he was dissuaded from entering the priesthood. His disappointed father sent him to medical school at Owens College, Manchester, but over the next six years, Francis failed to pass the exams. When his father cut off financial support, Thompson moved to London, where he became a homeless vagabond, addicted to opium and sleeping on the streets. He was rescued and cared for by Wilfred and Alice Meynell. He produced three volumes of poetry before dying of tuberculosis at age 48.

The Kingdom of God
"In no strange land"

O world invisible, we view thee,
O world intangible, we touch thee,
O world unknowable, we know thee,
Inapprehensible, we clutch thee!

Does the fish soar to find the ocean,   5
The eagle plunge to find the air—
That we ask of the stars in motion
If they have rumour of thee there?

Not where the wheeling systems darken,
And our benumbed conceiving soars!—   10

The drift of pinions, would we hearken,
Beats at our own clay-shuttered doors.

The angels keep their ancient places;—
Turn but a stone and start a wing!
'Tis ye, 'tis your estrangéd faces,   15
That miss the many-splendoured thing.

But (when so sad thou canst not sadder)
Cry,—and upon thy so sore loss
Shall shine the traffic of Jacob's ladder
Pitched betwixt Heaven and Charing Cross.   20

Yea, in the night, my Soul, my daughter,
Cry—clinging Heaven by the hems;
And lo, Christ walking on the water
Not of Gennesareth, but Thames!

The Poetry

Thompson maintains that the kingdom of God is not found in a strange land far off in the universe but is among us. In the first stanza, Thompson employs the device of oxymoron (apparent contradiction) to describe the kingdom: the adjectives are contradicted by the subsequent verbs in lines 1–4.

Similarly, the second stanza consists of three rhetorical questions to which the implied answer is no. Then in the third stanza, we are directed away from seeking answers by having "our benumbed conceiving" soar into astronomical space. From within "our own clay-shuttered" bodies, we can sense the presence of angelic "pinions" (wings, an image which continues the soaring motif) if we would listen and look.

Nevertheless, that discovery can cause a supremely depressing awareness of how far we are from the divine, a depression relievable only by crying out to God. The cry will be answered for Thompson with a new vision of Jacob's ladder descending to Charing Cross in London where he lives and with a vision of Christ now walking on the Thames. Thus the intangibles and vastness of outer space referred to early in the poem have been replaced with recognizable particulars.

The Piety

Pascal is credited with saying that there is a God-shaped vacuum in every human being that only God himself can fill. Thompson's poem bears witness to the truth of that observation but not in an entirely comforting way, for his advice is to seek the God within rather than the God without. This is a familiar theme in early Christian mysticism, whether we consult the writings of Julian of Norwich or Hildegard of Bingen. Yet Thompson does not simply extol the inward and introspective practice that is associated more with Buddhism than with Christianity. He uses the language of vision. A vision is indeed an internal experience, but its stimulus is from without, from a revelation from God. Therefore, Thompson alludes to Jacob's vision of the ladder and the vision of Christ walking on the water. Like so many of these visions, however, revelation condescends to the context of the visionary. In Thompson's case, Jacob's ladder appears not at Bethel but at Charing Cross in London, and Jesus is seen walking not on the Sea of Galilee but on the River Thames.

The message becomes clear. In our despair, God seeks us out where we live and speaks to us in a language or vision that we can grasp so that we need not miss "the many-splendoured thing" or its significance. But Thompson also knows that vision is not enough to fill the God-shaped vacuum in our souls. Only God can do so. Thus, the poem ends not with a glimpse of glory or a vision of angels but with Christ coming in person to the author. In the end, this alone is sufficient solace for the soul "clinging [to] Heaven by the hems."

Questions for Reflection

In what ways do you view, touch, know, and clutch the kingdom of God in the world around you?

In what ways do you find it difficult to connect with heaven?

Meditate on one of the visions of God found in the Bible. How might God condescend to your context and change the vision for you today?

Prior to your Christian walk, what did you use to try to fill the God-shaped vacuum in your heart?

How has God filled that longing since you have become a Christian? Take time to thank God for these blessings.

The Hound of Heaven

I fled Him, down the nights and down the days;
  I fled Him, down the arches of the years;
I fled Him, down the labyrinthine ways
  Of my own mind; and in the mist of tears
I hid from Him, and under running laughter.   5
        Up vistaed hopes I sped;
        And shot, precipitated,
Adown Titanic[1] glooms of chasmed fears,
  From those strong Feet that followed, followed after.
        But with unhurrying chase,   10
        And unperturbèd pace,
    Deliberate speed, majestic instancy,[2]
      They beat—and a Voice beat
      More instant than the Feet—
  "All things betray thee, who betrayest Me."   15

        I pleaded, outlaw-wise,
By many a hearted casement, curtained red,
  Trellised with intertwining charities[3]
(For, though I knew His love Who followed,
        Yet was I sore adread   20
Lest, having Him, I must have naught beside);
But, if one little casement parted wide,
  The gust of His approach would clash it to.
  Fear wist not to evade, as Love wist to pursue.
Across the margent[4] of the world I fled,   25
  And troubled the gold gateways of the stars,
Smiting for shelter on their clangèd bars;
      Fretted to dulcet jars
And silvern chatter the pale ports o' the moon.[5]
I said to dawn, Be sudden; to eve, Be soon;   30
  With thy young skyey blossoms heap me over
    From this tremendous Lover!
Float thy vague veil about me, lest He see!
  I tempted all His servitors, but to find

1. Immense (the Titans were giants).
2. Insistence.
3. Like an outlaw, the poet fled divine love, hoping instead to find sympathy and kindness in the human heart.
4. Margin or boundary.
5. Agitated or shook the portals of the moon until they gave forth sweet sounds.

My own betrayal in their constancy,   35
In faith to Him their fickleness to me,
   Their traitorous trueness, and their loyal deceit.
To all swift things for swiftness did I sue;
   Clung to the whistling mane of every wind.
           But whether they swept, smoothly fleet,   40
       The long savannahs of the blue;
        Or whether, Thunder-driven,
      They clanged His chariot 'thwart a heaven
Plashy with flying lightnings round the spurn o' their feet—[6]
   Fear wist not to evade as Love wist to pursue.   45
       Still with unhurrying chase,
        And unperturbèd pace,
     Deliberate speed, majestic instancy,
       Came on the following Feet,
       And a Voice above their beat—   50
    "Naught shelters thee, who wilt not shelter Me."

I sought no more that after which I strayed
       In face of man or maid;
But still within the little children's eyes
      Seems something, something that replies: 55
They at least are for me, surely for me!
I turned me to them very wistfully;
But, just as their young eyes grew sudden fair
       With dawning answers there,
Their angel plucked them from me by the hair.   60
"Come then, ye other children, Nature's—share
With me," said I, "your delicate fellowship;
      Let me greet you lip to lip,
      Let me twine with you caresses,
        Wantoning   65
     With our Lady-Mother's vagrant tresses,
        Banqueting
     With her in her wind-walled palace,
     Underneath her azured daïs,
     Quaffing, as your taintless way is,   70
       From a chalice
Lucent-weeping[7] out of the dayspring."
        So it was done;
I in their delicate fellowship was one—

6. The sky was sparkling with lightning-like sparks struck out by their hooves.
7. Dripping luminous drops.

Drew the bolt of Nature's secrecies.   75
        I knew all the swift importings[8]
        On the willful face of skies;
        I knew how the clouds arise
        Spumèd[9] of the wild sea-snortings;
           All that's born or dies   80
           Rose and drooped with—made them shapers
Of mine own moods, or wailful or divine—
        With them joyed and was bereaven.
        I was heavy with the even,
        When she lit her glimmering tapers   85
        Round the day's dead sanctities.
        I laughed in the morning's eyes.
I triumphed and I saddened with all weather,
        Heaven and I wept together,
And its sweet tears were salt with mortal mine;   90
Against the red throb of its sunset-heart
        I laid my own to beat,
        And share commingling heat;
But not by that, by that, was eased my human smart.
In vain my tears were wet on Heaven's gray cheek.   95
For ah! we know not what each other says,
        These things and I; in sound *I* speak—
Their sound is but their stir, they speak by silences.
Nature, poor stepdame, cannot slake my drouth;
        Let her, if she would owe[10] me,   100
Drop yon blue bosom-veil of sky, and show me
        The breasts o' her tenderness;
Never did any milk of hers once bless
        My thirsting mouth.
        Nigh and nigh draws the chase,   105
        With unperturbèd pace,
        Deliberate speed, majestic instancy;
        And past those noisèd Feet
        A voice comes yet more fleet—
"Lo naught contents thee, who content'st not Me."   110

Naked I wait Thy love's uplifted stroke!
My harness piece by piece Thou hast hewn from me,

8. Meanings.
9. Like the spray cast up by waves.
10. Own.

And smitten me to my knee;
I am defenseless utterly.
I slept, methinks, and woke,   115
And, slowly gazing, find me stripped in sleep.
In the rash lustihead of my young powers,
I shook the pillaring hours[11]
And pulled my life upon me; grimed with smears,
I stand amid the dust o' the mounded years—   120
My mangled youth lies dead beneath the heap.
My days have crackled and gone up in smoke,
Have puffed and burst as sun-starts[12] on a stream.
Yea, faileth now even dream
The dreamer, and the lute the lutanist;   125
Even the linked fantasies,[13] in whose blossomy twist
I swung the earth[14] a trinket at my wrist,
Are yielding; cords of all too weak account
For earth with heavy griefs so overplussed.
Ah! is Thy love indeed   130
A weed, albeit an amaranthine[15] weed,
Suffering no flowers except its own to mount?
Ah! must—
Designer infinite!—
Ah! must Thou char the wood ere Thou canst limn with it?   135
My freshness spent its wavering shower i' the dust;
And now my heart is as a broken fount,
Wherein tear-drippings stagnate, spilt down ever
From the dank thoughts that shiver
Upon the sightful branches of my mind.   140
Such is; what is to be?
The pulp so bitter, how shall taste the rind?
I dimly guess what Time in mists confounds;
Yet ever and anon a trumpet sounds
From the hid battlements of Eternity;   145
Those shaken mists a space unsettle, then
Round the half-glimpsèd turrets slowly wash again.
But not ere him who summoneth
I first have seen, enwound

11. Like Samson when he pulled down the temple.
12. Bubbles.
13. Poetic imaginings.
14. My world, my life.
15. Immortal, from the name of a flower that was reputed never to fade.

With blooming robes, purpureal, cypress-crowned;[16]   150
His name I know, and what his trumpet saith.
Whether man's heart or life it be which yields
      Thee harvest, must Thy harvest fields
      Be dunged with rotten death?[17]

      Now of that long pursuit   155
      Comes on at hand the bruit;[18]
      That Voice is round me like a bursting sea:
        "And is thy earth so marred,
        Shattered in shard on shard?
      Lo, all things fly thee, for thou fliest Me!   160
      Strange, piteous, futile thing,
Wherefore should any set thee love apart?
Seeing none but I makes much of naught," He said,
"And human love needs human meriting,
      How hast thou merited—   165
Of all man's clotted[19] clay the dingiest clot?
      Alack, thou knowest not
How little worthy of any love thou art!
Whom wilt thou find to live ignoble thee
      Save Me, save only Me?   170
All which I took from thee I did but take,
      Not for thy harms,
But just that thou might'st seek it in My arms.
      All which thy child's mistake
Fancies as lost, I have stored for thee at home;   175
      Rise, clasp My hand, and come!"

      Halts by me that footfall;
      Is my gloom, after all,
Shade of His hand, outstretched caressingly?
      "Ah, fondest, blindest, weakest,   180
      I am He Whom thou seekest!
Thou dravest love from thee, who dravest Me."

16. The cypress symbolizes death and mourning.
17. Must people die spiritually as well as physically in order to nourish their salvation?
18. Noise or din.
19. Lumpish; without spark.

The Poetry

"The Hound of Heaven" is the best known poem by Francis Thompson. Its 182 lines are deployed in stanzas varying between six and fifty-nine lines, with equally varied rhyme schemes. The dominant image is that of Christ as a hunter and lover in pursuit of the speaker's soul. The theme of relentless pursuit is developed through a stream of images of cosmic space and speed, especially in the three stanzas ending at line 110.

The pace slows in lines 111–154 as the speaker acknowledges the worthlessness of his life. The divine voice that previously admonished the speaker in single lines at the end of the first three stanzas now rebukes him in lines 155–170, but it concludes compassionately in the final twelve lines. Individualistic as this poem is, its argument resembles seventeenth-century poems such as "The Collar" by George Herbert, and the diction in lines 16–18, for example, is reminiscent of Romantic poems such as Keats's "Eve of St. Agnes."

The Piety

There are various places in Scripture where God is depicted as a warrior pursuing a foe (e.g., the Song of Deborah in Judges 5). However, the dominant image is a different sort of pursuit, a relentless seeking and saving of the lost akin to the parable of the lost sheep in Luke 15:1–7. Of course, the speaker is fleeing this "Hound of Heaven," fearful that if he is caught he will have to give such total allegiance to the divine pursuer that he would not be allowed to have other loves or friends or pursuits (lines 20–21). As the poem makes evident, his is a vain fear, for this pursuer does not seek to take away blessings but to show what their ultimate source is. This becomes especially clear in the lines, "All which I took from thee I did but take, / Not for thy harms, / But just that thou might'st seek it in My arms" (lines 171–73).

Lest we think that the entire scenario of this poem seems improbable, with Christ depicted as both the wooer and hunter of humankind, it is well to remember the testimonies of people like C. S. Lewis. He attested to the divine pressure he felt, and on the day of his conversion, he proclaimed himself the most reluctant convert in all Christendom. Clearly, the model of joyful conversion is not the only model. Indeed, no two conversions are exactly the same. Some come into the kingdom kicking and screaming, and others come in trying to kick the door down. Thompson spends a good deal of time emphasizing the personal nature of the interchange between hunter and hunted. He reminds us that no two relationships, even those involving the divine and humans, are ever exactly the same. That is what makes them personal relationships.

Finally, it is worth pointing out how the coda-like verses that close each section of the poem with a quote from Christ indicate that what is true of the master is also true of his servants. What is good or evil for the one is also good or evil for the other. Indeed, Thompson comes to realize (line 179) that what seems to be a time of gloom in his life may actually be the protective shade of God's outstretched hand. When we see things from the divine perspective, even the difficult and painful experiences turn out to prove the accuracy of Paul's words when he declared, "We know that all things work together for good for those who love God, who are called according to his purpose" (Rom. 8:28).

Questions for Reflection

Have you ever been afraid and felt like you were running from God? What went through your mind during this time in your life?

One of the major images of God that modern people have is a God who winds up the universe and then passively leaves it to run on its own. This poem suggests that the opposite is true. God is dynamically involved in time and space, to the point of wooing and pursuing particular individuals. Try the following discipline. Tomorrow morning get up and ask yourself, *Where can I see God at work today?* Try to see his hand in your daily life.

The image of God as lover suggests a God who badly wants relationships with human beings. It also suggests a God who relates to us as persons, which is to say he has given us the freedom to respond either positively or negatively to his overtures. A love relationship cannot be coerced. Think about times in your life when you responded to God in a loving way. What prompted this? Meditate on those times, and consider how your life would have been different if you had chosen not to respond in that way.

SEVENTEEN

Lesbia Harford
(1881–1927)

Lesbia Harford (née Keogh) was born in Melbourne, Australia, where she attended convent schools and graduated from university. In order to understand the conditions of working women, she worked in a clothing factory and also became involved in radical and union politics, joining the Industrial Workers of the World. A practitioner of free love, she was briefly married.

I Am No Mystic

I am no mystic. All the ways of God
Are dark to me.
I know not if he lived or if he died
In agony.

My every act has reference to man.   5
Some human need
Of this one, or of that, or of myself
Inspires the deed.

But when I hear the Angelus, I say
A Latin prayer   10
Hoping the dim incanted words may shine
Some way, somewhere.

Words and a will may work upon my mind
Till ethics turn
To that transcendent mystic love with which   15
The Seraphim burn.

The Poetry

Each of these unusual quatrains opens with a ten-syllable iambic line that is rather conversational. This is followed by a four-syllable iambic line that contributes a deepening emotion to the stanza. That metrical pattern is repeated in lines 3 and 4, and the two short lines rhyme. Intensified by the repetition of *w,* *u,* and *t,* and by the extra syllable in the final line, the last quatrain proclaims how prayer and purpose may change the speaker's opening denial ("I am no mystic") to participation in a "transcendent mystic love."

The Piety

This is a poem about hope, the hope that somewhere out there is a God who listens to prayer. The poet hopes for a transformation of self through prayer so that she may be aglow with a transcendent love like the angels. In a God-haunted culture, this is the sort of prayer we would expect. The poet begins with denial of being a mystic, yet she longs for a mystical experience. She is entirely focused on the things of this world, yet she has an uneasy sense that there must be something more. That which triggers her soul to remember is a part of the Latin liturgy, specifically lines from the Eucharistic rite: "Therefore with all the company of angels and archangels we laud and magnify thy name crying, 'Holy, holy, holy. God of power and might. Heaven and earth are full of thy glory. Glory be to thee, O God, most high.'"

Christian mysticism has a long tradition, and it is interesting that some of its most notable practitioners have been women (e.g., Julian of Norwich and Hildegard of Bingen). Mysticism is a form of religion that focuses on experience and often includes visionary experience. Harford is a person who longs to be a mystic. Indeed, it is often music or a familiar part of the liturgy that triggers or prepares the soul for a mystical experience. Consider, for example, the narrative in Revelation 1 where John says he was worshipping on a Sunday ("I was in the spirit on the Lord's day . . . ") when he suddenly had an overwhelming auditory and visual experience.

There is then a lesson to be learned from this poem. It helps to put ourselves in a place and frame of mind where we are open to the Almighty, receptive to the divine presence. We cannot compel such experiences, but we can prepare for them. So the poet makes room, hoping for an extraordinary encounter that will fill up the God-shaped and God-haunted vacuum in her soul.

Questions for Reflection

Are there special places where you can be close to God? What is the nature of these places?

Have you ever had a mystical or visionary experience of God? Did you write about this experience? If not, review the experience now, and write down your impressions, describing the content and nature of the experience.

What advice would you give to those searching for an encounter with God? Where would you tell them to look, and how would you instruct them to prepare?

EIGHTEEN

T. S. Eliot
(1888–1965)

After growing up in St. Louis and earning two degrees at Harvard, T. S. Eliot went on a fellowship to Germany in 1914. Following the outbreak of the First World War, he moved to Oxford. He became a British citizen in 1927 and declared himself to be "classicist in literature, royalist in politics, and Anglo-Catholic in religion."

In *The Waste Land* (1922), Eliot portrayed the loss of spiritual values in the modern world. His subsequent works regularly reflect his Christian beliefs and include poetry (*The Hollow Men* [1925], *Journey of the Magi* [1927], *Ash Wednesday* [1930], *Four Quartets* [1935–42]); plays (*Murder in the Cathedral* [1935] and *The Cocktail Party* [1950]); and prose (*For Lancelot Andrewes* [1928] and *The Idea of a Christian Society* [1939]). He became the most influential poet of his time.

Journey of the Magi

"A cold coming we had of it,
Just the worst time of the year
For a journey, and such a long journey:
The ways deep and the weather sharp,
The very dead of winter."   5
And the camels galled, sore-footed, refractory,
Lying down in the melting snow.
There were times we regretted
The summer palaces on slopes, the terraces,
And the silken girls bringing sherbet.   10

Then the camel men cursing and grumbling
And running away, and wanting their liquor and women,
And the night-fires going out, and the lack of shelters,
And the cities hostile and the towns unfriendly
And the villages dirty and charging high prices: 15
A hard time we had of it.
At the end we preferred to travel all night,
Sleeping in snatches,
With the voices singing in our ears, saying
That this was all folly.   20

    Then at dawn we came down to a temperate valley,
Wet, below the snow line, smelling of vegetation;
With a running stream and a water-mill beating the darkness,
And three trees on the low sky,
And an old white horse galloped away in the meadow.   25

Then we came to a tavern with vine-leaves over the lintel,
Six hands at an open door dicing for pieces of silver,
And feet kicking the empty wine-skins.
But there was no information, and so we continued
And arrived at evening, not a moment too soon   30
Finding the place; it was (you may say) satisfactory.

    All this was a long time ago, I remember,
And I would do it again, but set down
This set down
This: were we led all that way for   35
Birth or Death? There was a Birth, certainly,
We had evidence and no doubt. I had seen birth and death,
But had thought they were different; this Birth was
Hard and bitter agony for us, like Death, our death.
We returned to our places, these Kingdoms,   40
But no longer at ease here, in the old dispensation,
With an alien people clutching their gods.
I should be glad of another death.

The Poetry

This 1927 poem, the first in a series known as the Ariel Poems,
relates to Eliot's declaring himself "Anglo-Catholic in religion"
in the preface to *For Lancelot Andrewes* (1928). Bishop Andrewes
(1555–1626) was famous for his sermons, and two sentences

from his sermon for Christmas Day 1622 provide Eliot with the first five lines of the poem. These are modified from third person into first person, the speaker being one of the magi.

The poem is in free verse, with varying line lengths that reflect the rhythms of spoken phrases. The arrangement of lines 33–35 appropriately places extra emphasis on the repeated word "this," since "this" is the central question: "Were we led all that way for / Birth or Death?"

The first verse paragraph describes the hardships of the journey. The second contains several evocative images on which Eliot later commented in *The Use of Poetry and the Use of Criticism* (1933):

> [F]or all of us, out of all that we have heard, seen, felt, in a lifetime . . . certain images recur, charged with emotion. The song of one bird, the leap of one fish, at a particular place and time, the scent of one flower. Six ruffians see through an open window playing cards at night at a small French railway junction where there was a water mill. . . .

The "three trees on the low sky" (line 24) anticipate the crucifixion. Grover Smith writes of lines 26–28,

> Here are allusions to the Communion (through the tavern "bush"), to the paschal lamb whose blood was smeared on the lintels of Israel, to the blood money of Judas, to the contumely suffered by Christ before the Crucifixion, to the soldiers casting lots at the foot of the cross, and, perhaps to the pilgrims at the open tomb in the garden.[1]

The final verse paragraph presents an aged magus whose visit to the Christ child affected him deeply. Although he feels alienated from his countrymen and their beliefs, he has been unable to grasp the connection between the incarnation and the redemptive sacrifice of the crucifixion, and he ends yearning for his own death.

The Piety

In the first portion of this poem, the wise men offer up a litany of complaints that might well have been found on the lips of the

---

1. Grover Smith, *T. S. Eliot's Poetry and Plays: A Study in Sources and Meanings* (Chicago: University of Chicago Press, 1956), 124.

Israelites wandering in the wilderness. Instead of purity and
light accompanying the magi, their trip was characterized by
bad weather, ornery transportation, inhospitable rest stops, sordid conversations, questionable encounters, and ridicule. This is
not the stuff of the Christmas song "We Three Kings of Orient
Are," but it is likely nearer to the truth.

As it turned out, the good news of birth was the death knell for
all things dark and dangerous, all things sordid and sorry. In
short, the birth signaled the death of the old era through which
the magi had suffered to get to the manger. The birth left the magi
dissatisfied with the old dispensation and longing for its death.
Yet the birth also meant hard and bitter agony, for it was difficult
for even wise men to let go of "our places," "these Kingdoms."

The spokesman for the magi says he would certainly do it all
again. Even so, many years later he is still pondering whether he
had been called to witness a newborn wonder or a wake. This
birth left him questioning the difference between birth and
death. An anonymous poet once wrote, "Life and death upon one
tether . . . and running beautiful together."

The second stanza deliberately juxtaposes images that suggest
"in the midst of life, comes death." Lush vegetation is mentioned
as well as three cross-like trees. There is gambling for silver that
resembles Judas's gambit, but there was no information to be
learned from such chance encounters. Had they come too late
and arrived after the boy king had been executed? Or was the
end just plain from the beginning? Eliot leaves the door open for
speculation. But one thing he makes clear—once we have en-
countered the peace that passes understanding, we can only feel
uneasy in a world that is its antithesis. Things will never again
be the same.

Questions for Reflection

How does this description of the magi's journey affect your understanding of their part in the Christmas story?

What signs of the "old dispensation" are evident in your neighborhood?

What signs of the new life are evident?

How do birth and death come together in Christ's coming?

Do you personally need to experience more death of the old or more
   birth of the new?

Choruses from *The Rock*

The Eagle soars in the summit of Heaven,
The Hunter with his dogs pursues his circuit.
O perpetual revolution of configured stars,
O perpetual recurrence of determined seasons,
O world of spring and autumn, birth and dying!   5
The endless cycle of idea and action,
Endless invention, endless experiment,
Brings knowledge of motion, but not of stillness;
Knowledge of speech, but not of silence;
Knowledge of words, and ignorance of the Word.   10
All our knowledge brings us nearer to our ignorance,
All our ignorance brings us nearer to death,
But nearness to death no nearer to God.
Where is the Life we have lost in living?
Where is the wisdom we have lost in knowledge?   15
Where is the knowledge we have lost in information?
The cycles of Heaven in twenty centuries
Bring us farther from God and nearer to the Dust.

The Poetry

In the opening section of this first chorus from *The Rock* (1934), the free verse lines create an effect of self-contained units in a chant or catechism. The passage emphasizes how "twenty centuries" of nature's repetitive patterns in the heavens and on the earth are meaningless without an awareness of the "stillness," the "silence," "the Word" that is God. He is the unmoved mover who is both inside and outside time.

The repetition of "O" at the beginning of lines 3–5 and of the words "endless," "lost," "death," and "knowledge" (especially when the last is paradoxically equated with ignorance), helps to prepare for the pessimistic pronouncement in the final line. The energy and beauty of the opening two lines have dwindled into that ominous last word, "Dust." As Eliot had written in the section of *The Waste Land* titled "The Burial of the Dead," "I will show you fear in a handful of dust."

The Piety

This poem seems strangely prophetic of where we find ourselves at the turn of the millennium—lost in a morass of information thanks to the Internet, computers, smart calculators, voicemail, email, and the like. There is a strong sense of despair about being lost in the endless cycle of information, caught up in a spiral of words that keeps moving faster and faster. More to the point, so much of the information is useless, pointless, and downright counterproductive. Eliot depicts a secular society that knows a lot about a lot but very little about the Word that has eternal significance. He portrays the Word as something that breaks the endless cycle of yet more words, for it brings not just information but transformation.

There is a sense here that we are revisiting the Tower of Babel. Now we are duped by the notion that more knowledge will make us more godlike. On the contrary, suggests Eliot. Knowledge of something other than the Word can actually lead one away from God and toward a more secularized existence. It can lead to the illusion that we are the masters of our own fates, the captains of our own ships.

As mentioned above, the last line of the poem points to the dust of death. All this knowledge leads to death rather than life; it is death-dealing rather than life-giving. This attitude is similar to that in the Book of Ecclesiastes, where the knowing but jaundiced sage declares that life is vanity. Everything, including the pursuit of knowledge, leads to death. Nevertheless, Eliot's poem contains a glimmer of hope, for the author clearly believes that knowledge of the Word and a closer relationship with God is a possible, desirable, attainable goal. We see a poet profoundly sensitive to the spirit of his age, clinging to the Rock and hoping the sea of information either recedes or is transformed.

Questions for Reflection

   What endless cycles in your life cause distraction and distance you from God?

   How much time do you spend each day reading the paper? Surfing the web? Watching TV? Reading your Bible? Ask God to help you make his priorities yours.

   Read Psalm 119:89–96. Contrast the psalmist's point of view with today's culture.

   Take a few minutes to explore the knowledge of stillness and silence. Empty your mind of distractions, and ask God to fill the silence with his wisdom.

NINETEEN

C. S. Lewis
(1898–1963)

Clive Staples Lewis was born in Northern Ireland, served in the trenches in the First World War, and by 1925 had been appointed a fellow of Magdalen College, Oxford. He retained that position until 1954, after which he became professor of medieval and renaissance literature at Cambridge. At Oxford, Lewis, J. R. R. Tolkien, Charles Williams, and others, who became known as the Inklings, met to share their writing and religious explorations. Lewis became a popular lecturer and writer on religious and moral issues with books such as *The Screwtape Letters*, the Space Trilogy, and the Chronicles of Narnia. He recounts his loss and recovery of faith in the autobiographical *Surprised by Joy* (1955).

The Apologist's Evening Prayer

From all my lame defeats and oh! much more
From all the victories that I seem to score;
From cleverness shot forth on Thy behalf
At which, while angels weep, the audience laugh;
From all my proofs of Thy divinity,   5
Thou, who wouldst give no sign, deliver me.

Thoughts are but coins. Let me not trust, instead
Of Thee, their thin-worn image of Thy head.
From all my thoughts, even from my thoughts of Thee,
O thou fair Silence, fall, and set me free.   10
Lord of the narrow gate and the needle's eye,
Take from me all my trumpery lest I die.

The Poetry

As the title suggests, C. S. Lewis wrote this poem late in his life. Each stanza is composed of three couplets, expressing one of his deepest concerns: however highly he might be regarded as a scholar, writer, and lecturer, without God's grace he is unworthy and lost. In the third couplet, he goes so far as to dismiss his well-known works of Christian apologetics (such as *The Screwtape Letters*) because they lack a "sign" of God's approval.

In the second stanza, Lewis uses the metaphor of a ruler's image on a coin being a "thin-worn" imitation of the real person to demonstrate the discrepancy between his idea of God and the reality of God. Then, playing on the idiomatic phrase "silence fell," Lewis appeals to God as "thou fair Silence" to fall upon him and free him from his inadequate concepts of the divine.

In the final couplet, which appeals to Christ as the keeper of the "narrow gate and the needle's eye" (Matt. 7:13–14; 19:24), Lewis disparages his concept of God as mere "trumpery" that cannot save him.

The Piety

The Lewis we find in this poem is a chastened Lewis who has learned (at some cost) not to fall in love with his own words about the Lord but with the Lord himself. There comes a time when we need to be set free from our triumphs for God and even our clever or brilliant thoughts about God in order to be weaned of our pride in such things. Our personal salvation is not a result of what we have accomplished or fancy we have accomplished for the kingdom. Indeed, salvation may come in being delivered *from* our accomplishments, lest we fail to squeeze through the narrow gate due to being puffed up by hubris.

Lewis is also sanguine of the fact that what often entertains or enlightens the masses may in fact make heaven weep. As I once wrote:

> God's ways are not our ways,
> Our eyes cannot see,
> The logic of Love,
> Nailed to a tree.

Lewis also comes to grips with the fact that while God may give him no sign of pleasure or displeasure, God is still the deliverer to whom Lewis prays. Like Elijah who prays to die but does not take his own life, Lewis rests even his seeming triumphs in God's hands, trusting God to take away his "trumpery" and leave him to carry on in the divine-human encounter. In a sense, this is the ultimate act of faith: even when we despair of our own efforts and see through our false pretenses and God remains silent, we still pray and leave the results of our labor in God's hand. Lewis does so in this prayer and shows himself amid doubt and despair to be a true man of faith.

Questions for Reflection

In what aspects of your Christian walk are you particularly successful? Ask God to prevent you from being puffed up by pride as a result of these accomplishments.

Can you recall any times when you may have made your audience laugh, yet heaven wept at your actions? Take time now to repent of these actions if you have not already done so.

Have there been times when you have trusted more in philosophies about God than in God himself?

Take a few moments now to reflect in silence, asking God to help you refocus not on your own accomplishments or on philosophies but on his power.

TWENTY

F. R. Scott
(1899–1985)

Francis (Frank) Reginald Scott was the sixth son of Frederick George Scott, rector of St. Matthew's (Anglican) Church in Montreal, who served as a chaplain to the Canadian forces in the trenches of World War I. Frank distinguished himself as a crusading lawyer in Quebec, as dean of McGill University Law School, and as a founder and president of the political party that became the New Democratic Party of Canada. Amid all this public involvement, he remained a productive poet and often experimented with new forms.

Diagonals: Hands

hammer　in　whose　hands
these　wounded　gods
glittering　fastening
nails
driving　into
arms　open　the
cross　forever　upon　sky

The Poetry

One of two poems simply titled "Diagonals," "Hands" can be read from several directions: horizontally from left to right; diagonally from top left to bottom right; and diagonally from bottom left to top right. The cruciform shape of this crucifixion

141

poem is reminiscent of the cross of St. Andrew as it appears in the flag of Scotland.

In this ingeniously compact poem, individual words take on unusual force from their placement and spacing. Human hands wounded God's hands. The impact of nails being driven into Christ's outstretched arms is reinforced by the three participles that end in "-ing." Yet that destructive action forever opens the cross with its promise of salvation.

The Piety

Here indeed is a poem that comes to grips with the paradox of the cross. From one angle, the cross looks like an unmitigated disaster as an innocent person suffers capital punishment in the most humiliating form possible. It seems to demonstrate that there is no all-powerful God who is also all-good. The cry of Jesus—"My God, my God, why have you forsaken me?"—seems to go unanswered.

From another angle, however, this act of violence is seen as the ultimate act of peacemaking, reconciling God and humankind by means of Jesus' atoning death on the cross. Moreover, it demonstrates how God remains both just, punishing the world's sins, and loving, justifying ungodly human beings.

If we read the poem diagonally from top left to bottom right, the act of crucifixion is an attack on God, for it reads "hammer these glittering nails into the sky." Attempting to evacuate the world of the divine presence is the ultimate act of human perfidy. God is the heavenly Father, so an assault on the heavens ("sky") is an assault on him. It is the classic act of hubris to think God could be sent packing or be eliminated altogether by a human act. If humans wish to be gods in their own world, then God must die. The cross tells us as much about human fallenness as about divine grace and justice.

If, however, you read the poem diagonally from bottom left to top right, a slightly different point emerges: "cross arms driving nails fastening God's hands." The cross is not an attempt to eliminate God but to pin him down, to limit him, to put him in his place. This act is being undertaken by "cross arms" which could be interpreted as angry persons hammering furiously. God belongs on a cross, in a church, in a confined and restricted space to be determined by angry human beings. This is indeed the way many human beings feel about God. They become angry when God abandons sacred space and meddles in their personal lives.

The reference to "God's hands" reminds us that it is God incarnate we are referring to, namely Jesus. So perhaps we may say that the real issue is that God has come too close. He has invaded human space. He has threatened to take over the human domain. And so he must be pinned down again and put in his place. Of course, this is what the authorities tried to do to Jesus of Nazareth. They were constantly seeking to marginalize him, to put him in his place. When these efforts failed, they tried to eliminate him altogether. In the words of a popular song by Larry Norman, "They nailed him to the cross, they laid him in the ground, but they really should have known you can't keep a good man down."

If you read the poem horizontally, however, a more disjointed and postmodern sort of message comes across. Suddenly "God's" becomes a reference to "gods," and we realize we are no longer in a Christian world, reading things with Christian eyes. But they are wounded gods, and the reference could be interpreted as human beings. It is the wounded gods who hold the hammer. They are driving glistening nails into arms because the crucified one has offended or wounded their own sense of divinity, their own sense of power and autonomy. Paradoxically, while they may have thought to eliminate God so they can go on being gods (albeit vulnerable and wounded) in their own little world, what they have actually done is to "open the cross forever upon sky." Once set up, the cross cannot be taken down. Forever it stands as the bridge between heaven and earth, between God and humankind. Redemption once wrought cannot be erased. The bridge once built cannot be destroyed. The crucifixion opened a door that cannot be shut. It was done in public, in plain view and cannot be gainsaid or eliminated by mere human denial. Divine deeds cannot be erased by human words or willful human acts. This poem is a paradox, but it reflects the paradox that is at the heart of the universe, at the foundations of meaning.

Questions for Reflection

Have you ever been angry with God? Do you ever wonder how you would have reacted to Jesus if you had lived during his earthly life? If you had been a Roman soldier at the time, how do you think you would have reacted to the order to crucify Jesus?

Have you ever considered the cross from multiple angles before? How does the cross look from the point of view of God the Father? How did the cross appear to Jesus when he was enduring it? What do you think the women disciples who witnessed the crucifixion would have thought?

Take some time to reflect on the paradox at the heart of the divine-human relationship. Write about why you think God chose to bring about human redemption by this means. How does the cross reflect both God's justice and his mercy?

TWENTY-ONE

Langston Hughes
(1902–67)

Langston Hughes was born in Joplin, Missouri. After a child-hood divided between his separated parents, Hughes eventually became an outstanding figure in the Harlem Renaissance. Successful in several genres, he incorporates the rhythms and refrains of jazz and blues in his poems.

Ballad of Two Thieves

When Jesus died at Calvary
For what our world believes,
On either side upon a Cross
They hung two thieves—

Two members of a lowly mob   5
Who stole to get their bread
Were tied upon a Cross that day
To taste of death instead.

One thief looked at Christ and said,
If you're so great   10
As your followers swear—
Save yourself! Save me!
And save my brother thief there—
If you're as great
As your followers swear!   15

But he did not speak for his brother thief
Hanging on the gallows tree,

145

For the other thief cried only,
Lord, remember me!

Christ had the thorns upon His head   20
And in His mouth was gall.
From His palms the blood ran red
And on the ground did fall.

For the sins of man I suffer.
For the sins of man I die—   25
My body and my blood
Are the answer to your cry.

In the garden one betrayed me,
And Peter denied me thrice
But you who cry, Remember me!   30
Go with me to Paradise.

The Poetry

Hughes's choice of the ballad form is appropriate for his treatment of the crucifixion. Ballads traditionally recount tales of violence and death and the supernatural. Except for the third stanza, he uses ballad-like quatrains rhyming *abcb*, the second and fourth lines having fewer syllables than the first and third. Colloquialisms—"a lowly mob," "If you're so great"—add a modern flavor without detracting from the solemnity of the event.

The Piety

We are told from the outset that Jesus died "for what our world believes." This may refer to the fact that our world does not believe love is more powerful than hate and life is more powerful than death. In any event, it sets up a hostile atmosphere for the ensuing discussion between Jesus and the thieves. Hughes speculates that the two thieves are being crucified for stealing a crust of bread. However, the Greek text of this story in Luke 23:32 refers to them as evildoers or criminals, and we know from history that the Romans did not crucify people for petty theft. Yet in the poem neither of these men acts like a real malefactor.

A further liberty Hughes takes with the text is having one of the thieves offer the speech attributed to the Jewish leaders in

Luke 23:35 instead of taunting Jesus as recorded in Luke 23:39. The effect is quite dramatic. Rather than a taunt, we have a plea for salvation on behalf of both thieves, as well as an admission that the thief is not one of Jesus' followers. This is contrasted with the word of the other thief who simply says "Remember me." The rebuke of the second thief to the first and his additional words "when you come into your kingdom" are omitted.

Christ's response is likewise transformed. Instead of, "Today you will be with me in Paradise," we are told that the death of Christ is the answer to the cry, "Remember me!" Of course, this is precisely the deeper meaning of the story. There is also the suggestion here that we need only to cry out to Christ as the thief did to be assured a place in paradise. Salvation, then, hinges on the action of Christ on the cross and the willing response to it, coupled with a longing to "be in that number." Thus, Hughes effectively juxtaposes the injustice of humanity with both the justice and mercy of God.

Christ died for the sins of humankind and paid our debt to God. Yet in this same event, we see the mercy of God, because it was Christ instead of us on the cross. Furthermore, as Hughes emphasizes in the last stanza, Christ did this in spite of the fact that he was betrayed, denied, and deserted by his inner circle of disciples. Clearly, his act was one of pure grace. Not even the disciples who followed Jesus throughout his earthly ministry deserved salvation. Perhaps the old hymn writer expresses this idea best: "Two great wonders I confess. Your great grace, and my unworthiness." But then that is the very nature of Christ's grace—it is undeserved benefit, unmerited favor to us who with the thief are prepared to say, "Remember me."

Questions for Reflection

   What would you like your human legacy to be? For what do you wish to be remembered?

   Have you ever been betrayed? How did you react? Were you angry? Did you lash out?

   Which thief in the poem do you think you would more identify with?

   How do you react to Jesus' response at the close of the poem? Do you feel he is speaking to you?

TWENTY-TWO

Earle Birney
(1904–95)

Earle Birney was born in Calgary, Alberta, when it was still part of the Northwest Territories. He grew up on farms and worked as a forest laborer to earn money for college. After graduating from the University of British Columbia with honors in English, he did graduate work at Berkeley and Toronto, completing his Ph.D. at the latter with a dissertation on Chaucer's irony. Growing international tensions led him to join the Trotskyist faction of the Communist Party in 1933 (he interviewed Trotsky in Norway) and later to work for the International Labour Party in England. After serving in the Canadian Army during the Second World War, he taught at the University of British Columbia from 1948 to 1965, establishing Canada's first department of creative writing. Later, he served as writer-in-residence at several universities and became a world traveler. A highly versatile poet, Birney wrote in a great variety of traditional and experimental forms, including the omission of periods.

El Greco: *Espolio*

The carpenter is intent on the pressure of his hand
on the awl and the trick of pinpointing his strength
through the awl to the wood   which is tough
He has no effort to spare for despoilings
or to worry if he'll be cut in on the dice   5
His skill is vital to the scene   and the safety of the state
Anyone can perform the indignities   It's his hard arms
and craft that hold the eyes of the convict's women

There is the problem of getting the holes exact
(in the middle of this elbowing crowd)   10
and deep enough to hold the spikes
after they've sunk through those bared feet
and inadequate wrists he knows are waiting behind him

He doesn't sense perhaps that one of the hands
is held in a curious gesture over him—   15
giving or asking forgiveness?—
but he'd scarcely take time to be puzzled by poses
Criminals come in all sorts
as anyone knows who makes crosses
are as mad or sane as those who decide on their killings   20
Our one at least has been quiet so far
though they say he talked himself into this trouble
a carpenter's son who got notions of preaching

Well here's a carpenter's son who'll have carpenter sons
God willing   and build what's wanted   temples or tables   25
mangers or crosses   and shape them decently
working alone in that firm and profound abstraction
which blots out the bawling of rag-snatchers
To construct with hands   knee-weight   braced thigh
keeps the back turned from death   30

But it's too late now for the other carpenter's boy
to return to this peace before the nails are hammered

The Poetry

Birney imagines what is going through the mind of the carpenter depicted in the bottom right of El Greco's painting (which is reproduced on the cover of this book). Occasionally, the persona stands outside the carpenter (line 1 and lines 14–17), but the rest of the poem adopts the down-to-earth tone of the workman. The free verse, with spaces to imitate pauses for breathing or thinking, is well adapted to the subject.

The carpenter is proud of his workmanship, as lines 7–13 and 25–27 reveal. He has little respect for the actual executioners ("Anyone can perform the indignities") or the crowd (he "blots out the bawling of rag-snatchers"). His attitude to the victimized Christ is ambivalent. On the one hand, he professes indifference (lines 18–23). On the other, he shows sympathy for his "bared feet and inadequate wrists." Note the added force of "bared" as opposed to "bare." Later, he is glad that Christ "has been quiet so far" (line 21) and identifies with this other carpenter, whose fate he seems to regret in the last two lines of the poem.

The Piety

This brilliant poem is at its most fundamental level an irony or paradox. A carpenter is done in by a carpenter. A builder builds a structure to destroy the master builder. The poem then focuses on the periphery in El Greco's painting, bringing to its foreground the greatest paradox of all—the death of the one who is life, the destruction of the one who is creator, the end of the one who is eternal. As an anonymous poet once said, "Life and death upon one tether, and running beautiful together."

In both painting and poem, the carpenter focuses on the task at hand, while Jesus focuses on others' needs, indeed on the needs of the carpenter himself. As Birney suggests, Jesus' gesture of extending a hand over the carpenter suggests forgiveness or protection so the man may finish his work (see front cover). As is typical of El Greco paintings, Christ has an ethereal air. His face is turned toward heaven, and he appears to have glimpsed glory. But the carpenter sees none of this as he looks down at the wood and works. There is also a contrast between the serene Christ and the crowd grasping at his beautiful garment. Who is really being despoiled? Is it the crowd by their greed? Is it Christ by losing his garment? Or is it the carpenter, so focused on his task that he fails to see who is right in front of him? As the end of the poem suggests, a peace comes from being absorbed in work (a magnificent obsession, or better said, "a profound abstraction"), but it is not the peace that passes understanding.

Ever since Golgotha, people have been missing the tree for the forest. We miss Christ for the garment. We miss truth for the sake of beauty. We become so absorbed in our work that we miss glory as it goes by. Birney's poem raises two powerful questions: (1) What distracts us from looking squarely at the Christ, who is central to all human tableaus? (2) What lesser goods, such as work done well, prevent us from obtaining the highest good of all? Focal moments in life, which if ignored or overlooked, can later lead to the despairing cry, "The saddest words of tongue or pen, what might have been, what might have been." A life focused clearly on the divine-human encounter is one that can be lived without regret and without excuses. So, whether for the first or last time, we should look into the eyes of the figure at the center of this painting and ask ourselves, at what cost do we ignore him?

Questions for Reflection

Can you remember a time when you were so focused on your work that you missed something more important going on at the same time? What finally brought your attention to this other event?

What distractions in your life prevent you from looking squarely at Christ?

Focus for a few moments on the mental image of Jesus extending his hand of forgiveness over the carpenter. What emotions does this evoke in you?

What sins is Christ extending his hand over in your life? Ask God to help you see your sins and Christ's offer of forgiveness.

Take a few minutes to focus on the image of Christ on the cross and all that the scene entails physically, emotionally, and spiritually. Write about your reflections.

TWENTY-THREE

Richard Wilbur
(b. 1921)

Born in New York City, Richard Wilbur spent his childhood in North Caldwell, New Jersey. After graduating from Amherst College and Harvard University, he taught at several colleges before being appointed poet laureate of the United States in 1987. In addition to his carefully crafted poems, Wilbur's translations of plays by Molière and Racine and his lyrics for the musical *Candide* are greatly admired.

Matthew VIII, 28 *ff*.

Rabbi, we Gadarenes
Are not ascetics; we are fond of wealth and possessions.
Love, as you call it, we obviate by means
Of the planned release of aggressions.

We have deep faith in prosperity.   5
Soon, it is hoped, we will reach our full potential.
In the light of our gross product, the practice of charity
Is palpably inessential.

It is true that we go insane;
That for no good reason we are possessed by devils;   10
That we suffer, despite the amenities which obtain
At all but the lowest levels.

We shall not, however, resign
Our trust in the high-heaped table and the full trough.

152

If you cannot cure us without destroying our swine,   15
We had rather you shoved off.

The Poetry

Taking the story designated in the poem's title, Wilbur explores the character of the Gadarenes who, after Jesus saved two of them from demonic possession, were so ungrateful as to beg him to go away. Addressing Jesus as "Rabbi," the speakers of the poem engage in political and economic rhetoric and psychobabble that disguise their lack of humane feelings. A "planned release of aggressions" replaces "love," the existence of which they seek to deny. The second quatrain sounds like bureaucratic propaganda from George Orwell's *1984*, and it glosses over the fact that poverty still exists (lines 11–12). In the final quatrain, the diction bluntly descends to a swinish materialism and ingratitude. The tone of the poem is reinforced by the rhymes of the second and fourth lines in each quatrain.

The Piety

This poem will sound very familiar to those who have heard the current cultural mantra, "You only go around once in life. You'd better grab for all the gusto you can get." Though Christians may find it puzzling, some people are so materialistic and hedonistic that they have nearly deadened their consciences and squelched any feelings for other human beings. They attempt to rationalize their self-centered behavior. Even if they realize they are not well, they only want a cure if it allows them to continue pursuing the lifestyle they are accustomed to. They believe in the gospel of prosperity rather than the gospel of austerity. They would rather have pleasure than salvation, material benefits than eternal rewards. They can relate to the bumper sticker that proclaims, "He who dies with the most toys wins." Such is the posture of the Gadarenes in this poem—they are possessed by their possessions.

It is interesting to hear the rationalization they offer for their demon possession. We are told it happened for "no good reason." They cannot see that their lifestyle has led them down a dark and soul-destroying path. Ironically, these demoniacs are not delusional. They know they go crazy from time to time, but they have come to love their sickness more than they want a cure. They love their sin more than they want redemption. The demoniacs are obsessed with as well as possessed by their possessions. Hence, the last two lines emphasize their wish to keep their pigs instead of receiving a cure. In the end, they tell Jesus to shove off if he will not help them on their own terms. Like children who think God has not answered their prayers simply because the answer is no, the demoniacs can't imagine a blessing if it does not take the material form they desire. The rabbi's only possible response to such hard-hearted rudeness must be, "Thy will be done."

Questions for Reflection

It has been said that some people live to eat, and others eat to live. North Americans are often the worst offenders when it comes to the sin of gluttony. Take a moment to reflect on whether this may be an issue for you. Are you aware that many theologians have said overeating is a sin? Do you agree or disagree? Why or why not?

We live in what has been called a therapeutic culture, where a person's actions are all psychologized. People are not wicked, only sick and in need of counseling. What in the poem suggests such a perspective? Do you agree or disagree with this way of evaluating human behavior?

What is your perspective on demons? Do you believe the Gospel stories about demons are sometimes about mental illnesses? What would be the consquences for your approach to life if you really believed in a devil and demons?

TWENTY-FOUR

Vassar Miller
(b. 1924)

A lifelong resident of Houston, Texas, Vassar Miller was born with cerebral palsy. She earned B.A. and M.A. degrees from the University of Houston and has enjoyed a successful writing career. In 1961 she was nominated for a Pulitzer Prize in poetry.

Meditation after an Interview

I speak myself, and my name
is only smoke
and less than smoke.

I say who I am, and my name
slips from my mouth   5
to become a word in a foreign tongue.

I explain myself, and my name,
turned witness against me,
puts questions I cannot answer.

I say myself, and my name   10
drifts out, a bright colored bubble
to splinter against the wind.

But if You say me, my Lord, my name
I meet in Your darkness and hear it
singing content in Your silence.   15

The Poetry

Each of the first four stanzas begins with the speaker declaring who she is, reinforced by the insistent repetition of "and my name." But the images evoked in the second and third lines immediately deny her attempts to establish identity. She is as insubstantial as smoke or bubbles, as incomprehensible as a foreign tongue, as hostile as an interrogation in a court of law.

In the final stanza, the speaker addresses the Lord and imagines what his saying her name would mean—an experience that cannot be defined in material terms. Her speaking, saying, and explaining is transformed into singing. Individualistic assertion versus humble submission is reflected in the way this delicately shaped poem blends unrhymed lines of variable lengths in stanzas of consistent length.

The Piety

In today's culture, a name is often just a label. However, in the biblical tradition, a name conveys vital information about a person's nature, especially when it is God who names the person. This poem contrasts human attempts to establish identity with God's establishing a person in simply calling him or her by name.

Several biblical ideas underlie this poem. On the one hand, there is the prophetic assurance that not one word goes forth from God's mouth that is mere smoke. No word of God comes back to him null and void (Isa. 55:10–11). When God says something, that settles it. He is never a purveyor of empty rhetoric. If God calls people by name, then they must truly exist and matter. Indeed, they are established as persons of sacred worth, created in the image of God. God is prepared to have dialogues and relationships with them.

Miller also alludes to the Johannine tradition about Jesus as the great shepherd who calls his sheep by name (John 10:1–5). Notice how she breaks into song when she hears her name called by the one who really matters. Like a woman being told she has just conceived her first child after years of trying or a man being told he has just become a father for the first time, joy and doxology are the appropriate responses when God calls us by name.

Yet divine speech can take many forms, even silence. The rests in a divinely orchestrated concerto can speak as loudly as any C-major chord. The psalmist says, "Be still and know that I am God" (Ps. 46:10). Miller is learning that by being still rather than assertive, silent rather than vocal, she can hear the still small voice calling her by name.

The last line of the poem is a play on words. The poet is content in knowing that God has spoken her name. At the same time, God's speaking has given content and substance to her identity. When our lives are filled with content by God, even restless, self-assertive persons can be content with who they are and with their lot in life. The poem is titled "Meditation after an Interview." When that interview is with the Almighty, we come away knowing not only *who* we are but *whose* we are, and so we come to know our true names or identities.

Questions for Reflection

In what ways have you sought to establish your name or identity? Was this a satisfying or frustrating process?

What do you do when you feel that you are not truly appreciated for who you are? Do you pray about or have an interview with the Almighty? What has been the outcome of such sessions?

Have you ever audibly heard God speaking to you or believed strongly that he was speaking inwardly? How have you responded?

Why do you think so many people feel compelled to establish their names by means of self-promotion?

Do you think a person's good name matters, or should we not care what other people think about us? Write about this. Reflect on what it means to have God establish a person's name.

TWENTY-FIVE

Elizabeth Jennings
(b. 1926)

Born in Boston, Lincolnshire, Elizabeth Jennings graduated from the University of Oxford. She was made a Companion of the British Empire for services to poetry and was nominated for the post of poet laureate. A lifelong Roman Catholic, her poems address topics such as friendship, faith, and suffering, including her own mental breakdown, as titles of some of her volumes indicate: *The Mind Has Mountains* (a phrase from G. M. Hopkins's sonnet "No Worse, There Is None"), *Recoveries*, and *Moments of Grace*.

About writing poems, Jennings says, "If it goes well, it's surprisingly quick—maybe twenty minutes to half an hour. That's the most marvelous feeling. If I have a lot of trouble, it usually means that there's something wrong—you can't force a poem. . . . When a poem does come off, it's like grace: I don't feel it's any virtue of mine."

Meditation on the Nativity

All gods and goddesses, all looked up to
And argued with and threatened. All that fear
Which man shows to the very old and new—
All this, all these have gone. They disappear
In fables coming true,   5

In acts so simple that we are amazed—
A woman and a child. He trusts, she soothes.
Men see serenity and they are pleased.

Placating prophets talked but here are truths
All men have only praised   10

Before in dreams. Lost legends here are pressed
Not on to paper but in flesh and blood,
A promise kept. Her modesties divest
Our guilt of shame as she hands him her food
And he smiles on her breast.   15

Painters' perceptions, visionaries' long
Torments and silence, blossom here and speak.
Listen, our murmurs are a cradle-song,
Look, we are found who seldom dared to seek—
A maid, a child, God young.   20

The Poetry

In this poem, Elizabeth Jennings employs a rather unusual five-line stanza rhyming *ababa,* with the six-syllable fifth line sometimes linking into the next stanza. She treats the nativity of Christ as both a unique novelty and a fulfillment of long-held hopes and prophecies. All the superstitions and fears inherent in pagan mythologies are dispelled by the simplicity of this birth. The completeness of this change is emphasized by the five repetitions of "all" in the first stanza and the simplicity of the words, "A woman and a child. He trusts, she soothes."

The naturalness of the mother-infant relationship is reflected in many paintings of the infant at Mary's breast. Her innate modesty dismisses any embarrassment that witnessing breast-feeding might arouse. Other forms of imagining the nativity—dreams, legends, visionaries' accounts, murmurs—are at last happily fulfilled. They "blossom" and sing as we are urged to "listen" and "look" on the spectacle as defined in the last line with the striking simplicity of six monosyllables. This divine birth means that we who "seldom dared to seek" are "found." We have not done the finding; it is a gift to us.

The Piety

Jennings's poem captures many of the essential truths that we associate with the nativity. It is a story about innocence, purity, redemption, and relationship. It is a disclosure moment for the entire human race where we see all that we might be, how far we have to go, and how far we fall short of glory. It is much like naturalist John Muir said—we look at life from the backside of the tapestry. We normally see loose ends, knots, and dangling threads. However, occasionally the light shines through the tapestry, and we gain a glimpse of the larger design, the divine weaving together of darkness and light. All the loose ends are tied up, all the knotty problems are unraveled, and we are caught up in wonder, awe, and praise. Such a moment is the birth of Christ, where we see how "the hopes and fears of all the years are met in thee tonight."

Jennings makes a point much like that of J. R. R. Tolkien when she suggests that Christ's story is the fulfillment not only of prophecies but also of archetypal myths and deepest human dreams: "Lost legends here are pressed / Not on to paper but in flesh and blood" (lines 11–12). The birth of Jesus disarms our fears (line 2) and catches us up in amazement.

Nevertheless, there is more to this poem than just a reverie on the nativity. The poem goes on to speak of the fact that "God young" required nurture, indeed breastfeeding by Mary. Jennings emphasizes the intimacy of this relationship between Mary and her son, but she also conveys feelings of embarrassment to be observing such an intimate moment—like shepherds out of place. Yet it is no shame to witness this event, for Mary is not displaying herself for the world to see. Rather, she is fulfilling her role as mother. There is nothing unholy about such a thing, and even Jesus offers a smile of approval.

Jennings sees in the story of the nativity a convergence of all that is good and true and beautiful—everything that painters and visionaries have sought to express over the years. She sees us like the shepherds, swept up into the story as active witnesses to the greatest miracle of all. As Donne once wrote, "Twas much when man was made like God before; / But that God should be made like man—much more." Thus, we find ourselves singing a cradle song to Jesus, as if we had stepped into Mary's role. In fulfilling that role, we discover we have been found when we did not even know we were seeking. When his story becomes our story, we find ourselves part of God's larger design, threads in his tapestry of tragedy and triumph.

Questions for Reflection

Often when we think of Jesus, we see images of a compassionate man, the crucifixion, or a powerful Savior returning on a cloud. Take time now to call up images of babies—their innocence, neediness, playfulness, etc. Are these images new to your concept of a Savior?

Jennings says, "We are found who seldom dared to seek." How often do you seek God's presence?

The image of a breastfeeding child and its mother calls forth a tender portrait of intimacy between God and humanity. What is the level of intimacy in your relationship with Jesus?

How can you make your relationship with Jesus grow deeper?

TWENTY-SIX

Ted Hughes
(1930–98)

Growing up in rural Yorkshire, Edward James Hughes enjoyed hunting and fishing. Animals, birds, and fish figure prominently in much of his work, both for adults and for children. While completing a degree in archaeology and anthropology at Cambridge, Hughes met Sylvia Plath, the American poet with whom he was to have a troubled marriage. In 1984 he was appointed poet laureate of Britain.

Crow's Theology

Crow realized God loved him—
Otherwise, he would have dropped dead.
So that was proved.
Crow reclined, marvelling, on his heart-beat.

And he realized that God spoke Crow—   5
Just existing was His revelation.

But what
Loved the stones and spoke stone?
They seemed to exist too.
And what spoke that strange silence   10
After his clamour of caws faded?

And what loved the shot-pellets
That dribbled from those strung-up mummifying crows?
What spoke the silence of lead?

Crow realized there were two Gods—   15

One of them much bigger than the other
Loving his enemies
And having all the weapons.

The Poetry

"Crow's Theology" is a representative poem from Hughes's
volume titled *Crow: From the Life and Songs of the Crow* (1970).
This harshly compelling collection features the predatory crow,
which serves as a symbol for violent, genocidal humankind.

This poem mimics the pseudological questionings of one seeking to understand what God is. Crow's first realization, that
"God loved him," appears to prove the Christian message. The
second realization, that God exists and "spoke Crow," makes
God at least somewhat akin to Crow. What then serves as God
for stones, silence, and hanged crows? Then comes Crow's third
realization, that behind the loving God is an omnipotent God,
potentially capable of destroying those he loves. Unlike the reas-
suring first four lines, the last four lines are implicitly threaten-
ing and alarming. The conversational effect of the irregular lines
of free verse have a natural rhythm and reflect the speaker's sar-
donic attitude.

The Piety

Hughes's poem raises interesting questions about our per-
spectives on God. Since the perspective is that of a crow, however, the poem raises more questions about anthropology than
theology. By this I mean that creation looks different to those
who see human beings as created in God's image and believe the
world was made especially for them. In other words, a crow's
point of view may not be an accurate reflection on the nature of
God.

But let's suppose for a moment there is something to the
crow's reflections. We may need to be reminded that God's nature involves justice and mercy, holiness and love, passion and
compassion. This being so, it is often hard for human beings to
imagine all these qualities embodied in one being. This is in part

why pagans are polytheists. It is easier to believe in multiple gods with differing character traits than in one complex deity.

Nevertheless, since human beings created in God's image are themselves so complex, why should we imagine the one true God to be any different? Why should we assume that our inability to understand how God's justice and mercy can be reconciled means it cannot be so? Is the human mind the proper measuring rod for determining the coherency of the deity and his creatures? I suggest not, for there is a need for humans to suspend judgment about various things when our knowledge of God is so limited. If we take the crow's perspective into our hearts now, we may find ourselves eating crow later!

Questions for Reflection

Think for a moment of an occasion when you made a snap judgment about an important matter only to discover later you had misread the situation. How did you feel when you discovered you were wrong? Did you try to make amends, or did you cover things up?

Can you identify with Crow's perspective in this poem? It has been said that a Christian is called to have a simple faith but not a simpleton's faith. Which sort of faith do you think Crow exhibits?

How do you relate to our complex God when things don't seem to be going your way? Read Psalm 118, and reflect on this poem in light of it.

TWENTY-SEVEN

John Updike
(b. 1932)

John Updike grew up in the small town of Shillington, Pennsylvania, an experience reflected in his numerous novels and short stories. In his memoir "The Dogwood Tree," he explains that he saw writing "as a method of riding a thin pencil out of Shillington, out of time altogether, into an infinity of unseen and even unborn hearts. [I] pictured this infinity as radiant."[1] This vision coexists with his Christian faith.

Seven Stanzas at Easter

Make no mistake: if He rose at all
it was as His body;
if the cells' dissolution did not reverse, the molecules reknit,
    the amino acids rekindle,
the Church will fall.

It was not as the flowers,   5
each soft spring recurrent;
it was not as His Spirit in the mouths and fuddled eyes of the
    eleven apostles;
it was as His flesh: ours.

The same hinged thumbs and toes,
the same valved heart   10
that—pierced—died, withered, paused, and then regathered
    out of enduring Might
new strength to enclose.

1. John Updike, *Assorted Prose* (New York: Knopf, 1965), 185.

Let us not mock God with metaphor,
analogy, sidestepping, transcendence,
making of the event a parable, a sign painted in the faded
    credulity of earlier ages: 15
let us walk through the door.

The stone is rolled back, not papier-mâché,
not a stone in a story,
but the vast rock of materiality that in the slow grinding of
    time will eclipse for each of us
the wide light of day.   20

And if we will have an angel at the tomb,
make it a real angel,
weighty with Max Planck's quanta, vivid with hair, opaque in
    the dawn light, robed in real linen
spun on a definite loom.

Let us not seek to make it less monstrous,   25
for our own convenience, our own sense of beauty,
lest, awakened in one unthinkable hour, we are embarrassed
    by the miracle,
and crushed by remonstrance.

The Poetry

"Seven Stanzas at Easter" consists of seven quatrains in
which, unorthodoxly, the first and fourth lines rhyme. The un-
usually long third lines are another feature and are followed by
the short fourth lines, which give a sense of closure to each
stanza.

These departures from conventional form suit the speaker's
unconventional attitude toward Christ's resurrection. Updike re-
jects interpretations that prettify the resurrection and evade its
physical reality. The second and fourth stanzas cogently articu-
late his position. In emphasizing Christ's humanity, Updike employs terms from modern science: "cells," "molecules," "amino
acids" (line 3); "materiality" (line 19); and "Max Planck's quanta"
(line 23). This technique reinforces the sense that the topic is
being addressed with a scientist's professional seriousness. As he
maintains at the start of the sixth stanza, if we insist "we will

have an angel at the tomb" ("will" being a stressed syllable), it must be a real one.

The last stanza reiterates the speaker's argument. Updike's forcing "monstrous" to rhyme with "remonstrance" throws that final word into particular prominence. Among its meanings as illustrated in the *Oxford English Dictionary* are "evidence," "demonstration," and "a gesture of reproof." All these meanings are appropriate to the argument of this poem.

The Piety

It is normal in Christian circles to speak of the scandal of the cross, but Updike has chosen to speak about the scandal of the resurrection. The truth is, without the resurrection, the death of Christ would not have saving significance. The resurrection not only vindicates Christ and validates his claims but also sheds light on the real meaning of the cross and activates what it promises. Without the resurrection, Christ's death would have been just another human tragedy, ominous proof that Christ was indeed forsaken or even cursed by God as many early Jews believed about crucifixion victims.

Instead of making Christ a victim, the resurrection gives him victory over and beyond death. Precisely at this point, Updike emphasizes that reality beyond the grave is no less real and tangible than life on this side of the grave. Indeed, it is just as real and concrete, if not more so. Updike has no patience for those who wish to hide the scandal of the resurrection behind the word metaphor or parable. His point is simple: If we believe in the resurrection, let us not allow that belief to die the death of a thousand qualifications or equivocations. Either a full-blooded belief in the resurrection is necessary, or we should be done with the matter.

In the second stanza, Updike wishes to emphasize that resurrection is not like the cycle of crops. It is not merely life beginning again as it always does. Resurrection is about real life after real death. It is about God's yes to life being louder than death's no. It is about God miraculously having the last word, even in this vale of disease, decay, and death. In Updike's opinion, equating resurrection with crop cycles or myths of eternal return or metaphors is mocking God. Equating resurrection with such things also, according to the first stanza, undercuts the very foundation of the church. Updike suggests the church will fall without the resurrection. If Christ is now alive, the living Lord, then he is the head of the living body, the church. The church without a living head is indeed a fallen and dead entity.

Thus, the poem ends with a warning: Do not attempt to whittle away the hard edges of the resurrection for the sake of comfort or convenience in the scientific age. Indeed, the way Updike uses language suggests that since all truth is God's truth, including scientific truth, in the physical resurrection of Christ all truths converge. The poem concludes with a reminder of the final resurrection, when we will be awakened and asked to give an account of whether we were embarrassed by the Easter miracle or owned it. The final line suggests that when we experience our own resurrection, the ocular proof will provide a crushing demonstration that we were wrong about Christ's resurrection if we do not follow the poet's urging and "walk through the door" of the empty tomb into the realm of belief.

Questions for Reflection

Do you think science and faith are enemies or companions? Why?

Read 1 Corinthians 15:12–19. Compare Paul's and Updike's views of the importance of Christ's resurrection.

What do you think would happen to the church and in the church without belief in a bodily resurrection?

What does Updike mean by "sidestepping transcendence"?

How is the resurrection "monstrous"?

Is it difficult for you to believe in Christ's bodily resurrection? Why or why not? Take time to pray for God to increase your faith and understanding.

TWENTY-EIGHT

Peter Kocan
(b. 1947)

At the age of nineteen, Peter Kocan attempted to assassinate the leader of the Australian Labour Party and was sentenced to life imprisonment. During ten years in Morisset Mental Hospital, he wrote several semiautobiographical novels and poems. His later poems explore the difficulty, in the brutal modern world, of trying to recover religious faith.

Cathedral Service

I'm only here because I wandered in
Not knowing that a service would begin,
And had to slide into the nearest pew,
Pretending it was what I'd meant to do.

The tall candles cast their frail light   5
Upon the priest, the choir clad in white,
The carved and polished and embroidered scene.
The congregation numbers seventeen.

And awkwardly I follow as I'm led
To kneel or stand or sing or bow my head.   10
Though these specific rites are strange to me,
I know their larger meaning perfectly—

The heritage of twenty centuries
Is symbolised in rituals like these,

In special modes of beauty and of grace   15
Enacted in a certain kind of place.

This faith, although I lack it, is my own,
Inherent to the marrow of the bone.
To this even the unbelieving mind
Submits its unbelief to be defined.   20

Perhaps the meagre congregation shows
How all of that is drawing to a close,
And remnants only come here to entreat
These dying flickers of the obsolete.

Yet when did this religion ever rest   25
On weight of numbers as the final test?
Its founder said that it was all the same
When two or three were gathered in his name.

The Poetry

The apparent indifference behind the speaker casually entering the cathedral is conveyed by his defensive protest in the first line and his embarrassment at having "to slide into the nearest pew," pretending that he had come for the service. In the second quatrain, he absorbs the religious atmosphere, which is somewhat undermined by the presence of only seventeen in the congregation.

At the start of the third quatrain, "awkwardly" is indeed the way he follows the actions of the service as catalogued in the four verbs in line 10. In spite of his unfamiliarity with these "rites," however, he has inherited "their larger meaning" accumulated over two thousand years of Christian culture and reflected in the loftier language of the fourth quatrain.

The paradoxes in his attitude are further developed in the fifth quatrain: If belief did not exist, "unbelief" would be meaningless. In the sixth quatrain, the speaker speculates that the meagerness of the congregation is a symptom that Christianity is now obsolete. The final quatrain offers a rebuttal by referring to Jesus' declaration that two or three believers sufficed to establish a congregation. In doing so, Kocan creates a positive conclusion that is far different from his hesitant opening.

The Piety

Like the speaker in the poem by Harford discussed previously,
the main character in Kocan's poem would like to have faith but
is afraid that such faith, if not futile, is obsolete and ill-suited to
the modern world. Also similar is the shift from denial or doubt
to hopefulness as the speaker recognizes that not numbers but
the nature or character of the fellowship is what validates such
a faith.

Kocan illustrates the difference between personal faith in the
God of Christianity and a knowledge of what the faith is about,
perhaps even embracing it as a cultural heritage and legacy.
There is a sense in which this religion does not belong to the author. In fact, he belongs to it whether he wishes it or not. It is his
by inheritance and goes to the marrow of his being, even if he
has not embraced it as a personal possession.

The author finds the church and its ceremonies familiar, even
comfortable. Yet he is embarrassed to show up while a service is
in progress. Why is this? Is it because he is not on familiar terms
with the God being worshipped in the service? This seems to be
the case. Nevertheless, he knows that such worship can be real
or valid, even if only two or three are gathered in Christ's name.

Kocan raises the interesting question of what makes a faith
obsolete as opposed to just old. An obsolete faith is one that has
not stood the test of time and no longer kindles true worship and
real faith in the hearts of its adherents. By contrast, an old faith
can often accomplish both of these ends. There is also an important distinction between the form of faith (certain hymns,
prayers, and rituals) and the substance of faith. Sometimes the
form can become obsolete, but the substance is carried on in
new forms. The danger is in mistaking the form for the substance, and Kocan seems prone to it. In the end, however, there
is a wistfulness. When all is said and done, we get the feeling the
author would like to be reckoned among the faithful few.

Questions for Reflection

Have you ever felt that the worship service you were attending was
obsolete or unhelpful? Have you reflected on whether this has to
do with the substance or life of the service, or whether it has to do
with cultural preferences for a certain kind of music or ritual?

Write about your worship preferences, and then reflect on why you are inclined in the direction you are. Is there any biblical basis for your preferences?

Have you ever come into a worship service that was already in progress? How did you feel when you entered? Were you able to join in the act of worship, or did you feel like an outside observer?

Have you ever judged the validity of worship based on the number of people present? What is wrong with evaluating things in this manner?

Index